The Best Days of Our Lives

SCHOOLDAYS

compiled by
Gervase Phinn

First published in 2015 by Country Publications Ltd
The Water Mill, Broughton Hall
Skipton, North Yorkshire BD23 3AG
www.dalesman.co.uk

Text and editorial selection © Gervase Phinn 2015
Additional text © contributors listed on p159–160, 2015
Photographs © Getty Images 2015

ISBN 978-1-85568-347-1

Printed in China for Latitude Press Ltd.

Contents

INTRODUCTION

This book is an amazing compilation of childhood recollections, musings and experiences about children, teachers and schools from a wide range of people. There is humour, of course, but there is also pain and regret, triumphs and traumas. Some of the memories, I guess, will make you laugh out loud, others will sadden you; all will remind you of your own schooldays which I hope were the happiest days of your life.

Gervase Phinn

Dedication
For Geraldine Pick

Chapter One

THE GOOD OLD DAYS

Teachers have it too easy these days and no mistake.

You're right there. When I started teaching all I had was a stick of chalk and a board rubber.

You had a board rubber? I had to use my sleeve and I had to make the stick of chalk last all term.

The class had to share a pencil.

You had pencils? Mine wrote on slates.

I had fifty in my class.

Fifty! I had a hundred.

And there were no fancy trainers. They all wore clogs.

Clogs? They had clogs? Mine hadn't a shoe between them.

They had to walk three miles to school.

Walk! Mine had to run the five miles uphill all the way, climb three drystone walls and swim the beck.

They'd come to school with colds and flu.

I have never let my schooling interfere with my education. — Mark Twain

Mine had cholera.
>   *And we only had one football.*
Football! You were lucky. We used an inflated pig's bladder.
>   *If they didn't work they had to stand in a corner for the whole day with a*
>   *dunce's cap on.*
Mine were locked in the coal house for a week.
>   *They were so noisy I'd have to shout to make myself heard.*
Noisy! It was strict silence in my day. Anyone who spoke was sent to the
headmaster and was never seen again.
>   *If they misbehaved they got the cane.*
We used a piece of lead piping.
>   *We had it hard in those good old days.*
We did. Teachers today don't know they are born.

How many times do we hear the comment from a member of the older
generation that schools are not what they were? It is a commonly held view
that education was much better in the past — higher standards, rigorous
lessons, stricter teachers and well-behaved children.

Discipline in the Victorian classroom was indeed very strict. Children had
to stand up straight when an adult entered the room, boys holding their
hands clasped behind their backs and the girls with hands held together in
front. They had to wait for permission to speak, not ask questions, not raise
a hand unless they were told to do so. Should they talk or fidget, fail to pay

Too often we give children answers to remember

attention, play truant or arrive late for school they would be caned. If they produced substandard work they were made to stand in the corner wearing a dunce's cap.

In former times, lessons were hard and chastisement was severe. At Threshfield School, near Grassington in Wharfedale (founded in 1674), punishments included having to stand on one leg and hold at arm's length a heavy log, on which was carved a Biblical passage which had to be learnt by heart for the punishment to end. One boy, caught stealing berries, had to sew them back on to the bushes with needle and thread. Hard to believe, but it happened.

Oliver Goldsmith's description of the schoolmaster in *The Deserted Village* is not untypical:

The village schoolmaster taught his little school;
A man severe he was, and stern to view;
I knew him well, and every truant knew;
Well had the boding tremblers learned to trace
The day's disasters in his morning face.

One would think that with such strict discipline in the classroom that the pupils never stepped out of line. The old school log books, inspectors' reports and newspaper accounts, however, reveal a very different story, that the children could be far from hard-working and obedient. A log book of

rather than problems to solve. — Roger Lewin

1848 reveals that one boy was caned for throwing a chair at a teacher, another for setting fire to the outhouse, and two boys beaten for dumb insolence. Three children were expelled for pelting the teacher with stones and one boy was locked in the hen coop with all the dead hens which he had killed.

Report on the school attached to Bar Chapel, Cowling (1871):

Discipline at the school was so lax that occasionally on a very nice day they (the scholars) would stage a mass "walk-out", and prefer the pleasures of fresh air than the stuffiness of the school building.

The pupils are regularly in trouble with their teacher for incidents involving eye-gouging, elbowing, kicking, punching and over-vigorous rucking.

The charge per pupil was 3d per week. The lack of discipline resulted in frequent truancy, and the 3d being spent on sweets instead of education.

One pupil claimed that all he learnt to do at school was to draw horses on slates and roast apples on the school stove.

Report of E M Sneyd-Kynnersley HMI (1913):

My particular bugbear was a Manchester board school. During school hours there is seldom a lull in the infernal din.

For every student with a spark of brilliance, there are

Extract from the Keighley News *(May 30th 1925):*

Once a year the school broke into open rebellion. This happened on Royal Oak Day (May 29th) when the schoolmaster was held to ransom, and if he would not grant a day's holiday, was locked either in or out of the school. More than once, when his entrance was barred, he had to crawl in at the open window, and his dignity suffered in consequence. The scholars would at once unlock the door, and rushing out of the place, would play truant for the whole day.

A favourite form of punishment was to confine the delinquents to the coal-place, but invariably the tables were turned, for after filling the coal bucket the master would find himself locked in when the whole school would decamp into the woods and fields.

Despite school attendance being made compulsory for five- to ten-year-olds in 1880 this was not widely adhered to. One country school in Nottinghamshire recorded in 1883 the following reasons for absenteeism:

Turnip singling, carrot weeding, pea pulling, potato picking, wall building, goose plucking, inability to pay fees, bad feet, travelling circus, impassable road, harvest, beating for the squire's shoot.

There was no national curriculum in the early days, and little paperwork for the teacher to complete. The *Rules for Teachers* of 1844 listed the directives,

about ten with ignition trouble. — Milton Berle

Nothing grieves a child more than to study the wrong lesson

short and sweet, for schoolmasters and schoolmistresses:

To promote by precept and example cleanliness, neatness and decency;

To impress a time and a place for everything and everything in its proper place;

To treat pupils with kindness and firmness;

To keep a register, report book and class lists accurately and neatly;

To teach to the Board's schoolbooks.

The curriculum was narrow, consisting of reading, writing and arithmetic, religious education (Christian), a study of British history and world geography and some practical activities, usually needlework for the girls and technical drawing for boys. Things changed little over subsequent years, and until the Education Act of 1944 the subjects were still predominantly reading, writing and arithmetic. The boys were sometimes taught gardening and woodwork, the girls subjects like needlework, cooking and general housework. One morning every week they had a visit from the vicar who would take the classes for religious instruction.

Sir Alec Clegg, former Chief Education Officer of the West Riding of Yorkshire, lists some of the bizarre activities that happened in the classrooms of the past. His grandfather was a schoolmaster from 1869 until after the

and learn something he wasn't supposed to. — E C McKenzie

First World War, and during the time when he was at school, youngsters in their early teens had to learn by heart curious mathematical rules of this kind entitled 'Fellowship with Time':

> As the sum of the product of each man's money and time is to the whole gain or loss, so is each man's product to his share of the gain and loss. When these rules were put into practice the questions were asked, sometimes mixed with religion: There are 12 patriarchs, 12 apostles and 12 evangelists. Add the patriarchs and the evangelists together and subtract the apostles. What is the remainder?

From the Sir Alec Clegg Lecture, Bingley College, 1974

It was clear from the earliest commentaries of the school inspectors and the conclusions of the various national reports into the education of the young, that much of the work undertaken in schools was poor. The Newcastle Commission of 1862 was blunt in its conclusions:

> None (referring to teachers in private schools) are too old, too poor, too ignorant, too feeble, too sickly, too unqualified in one or every way, to regard themselves as to be regarded by others as unfit for school keeping. We have seen overwhelming evidence from Her Majesty's Inspectors, to the effect that not more than one fourth of the children receive a good education. Want of thoroughness and foundation; want of system; slovenliness and showy superficiality;

Children have more need of models than of critics. — Joubert

inattention to rudiments; undue time given to accomplishments, and those not taught intelligently or in any scientific manner; want of organisation — these may sufficiently indicate the character of the complaints we have received, in their most general aspect.

In every phase of secondary teaching, the first aim should be to educate the mind, and not merely to convey information. It is a fundamental fault, which pervades many parts of the secondary teaching now given in England, that the subject (literary, scientific or technical) is too often taught in such a manner that it has little or no educational value.

HMI Matthew Arnold was dismayed by what he observed:
A book is selected at the beginning of the year for the children of a certain standard; all the year children read this book over and over again, and no other. When the inspector comes they are presented to read in this book; they can read their sentence or two fluently enough, but cannot read any other book fluently.

A colleague's report of 1847 again touches on the subject of reading:
The singular slowness with which the children of our national schools learn to read, a fact to which all our reports have borne testimony, is in some degree attributed to the unwise concentration of the leaders of the school on that single subject.

There is only one thing that costs more than education, the lack of it. — Anonymous

Ragged bodies, matched by ragged minds, frail forms
sustained by slender resources, unshod feet little prepared at
eleven for the roughness of life's highway.

Charlotte Brontë in *Jane Eyre* describes the cruelty and neglect children
experienced in some Victorian schools. Her description of Lowood, a charity
school for girls to which young Jane is sent, is stark and harrowing. The eighty
pupils are subjected to cold rooms, poor meals and thin clothing. When Jane's
friend Helen Burns asks some slight question about her work she is 'chidden
for the triviality of the inquiry' by Miss Smith, her teacher. Poor Helen is con-
demned by Miss Scatcherd, another teacher, to a dinner of bread and water
because she had blotted an exercise in copying it out.

Mr Brocklehurst, 'the black pillar clergyman' and director of the Lowood
Institution, is harsh, malicious and hypocritical and makes Jane stand on a
chair all day for accidentally breaking a slate, but he does so after he has humil-
iated her before the whole school. 'You see she is yet young; you observe she
possesses the ordinary form of childhood; God has graciously given her the
shape that He has given to all of us; no single deformity points her out as a
marked character. Who would think that the Evil One had already found a
servant and agent in her? Yet such, I grieve to say, is the case.'

The description of the plight of children by Charles Dickens in his novels
changed the public perception of the treatment of children. They pricked

people's consciences and touched their hearts. His account of the lesson given by the odious Wackford Squeers, the headmaster of Dotheboys Hall in *Nicholas Nickleby,* offers us a salutary reminder that things were not quite as rosy in the good old days of education.

'This is the first class in English spelling and philosophy, Nickleby,' said Squeers, beckoning Nicholas to stand beside him. 'We'll get up a Latin one, and hand that over to you. Now, then, where's the first boy?'

'Please, sir, he's cleaning the back-parlour window,' said the temporary head of the philosophical class.

'So he is, to be sure,' rejoined Squeers. 'We go upon the practical mode of teaching, Nickleby; the regular education system. C-l-e-a-n, clean, verb active, to make bright, to scour. W-i-n, win, d-e-r, der, winder, a casement. When the boy knows this out of a book, he goes and does it. It's just the same principle as the use of the globes. Where's the second boy?'

'Please, sir, he's weeding the garden,' replied a small voice.

'To be sure,' said Squeers, by no means disconcerted. 'So he is. B-o-t, bot, t-i-n, tin, bottin, n-e-y, ney, bottinney, noun substantive, a knowledge of plants. When he has learned that bottinney means a knowledge of plants, he goes and knows 'em.'

---

think you've got more than you have. — Anonymous

Nowadays, when a speaker tells the graduates that the future is

Chapter Two

AND SO TO SCHOOL

FIRST DAY AT SCHOOL

'I do not want to go to school,
I'd rather stay in bed.
I know that I won't like it,
May I stay at home instead?

'I just won't like the teachers,
And all the girls and boys,
I'd sooner stay at home with you
And play with all my toys.'

'Now come along,' his mother cried,
'Let's have you out of bed.
You have to go to school today,
After all, you are the head.'

---

theirs … is that a promise or a threat? — Milton Berle

I am five. The photograph shows a chubby little boy with a round pale face, a mop of black hair and large eyes, standing on the back step of the house in Richard Road, taken just before he sets off for his first day at school. He does not look at all happy. In fact, he seems on the verge of tears. He is wearing a crisp white shirt and little tartan clip-on tie, short grey trousers which he eventually will grow into, socks pulled up to the dimpled knees and large polished black shoes and a blazer. A rose is pinned to his lapel.

When I look at the photograph I wonder just what my mother was doing sending me to school like a little adult attending a wedding. The class photograph, taken at the end of my first year, shows that my mother's taste in my clothes had not altered, for I am there again dressed like a little dandy. The girls are all dressed in similar clothes: pale cotton, knee-length dresses, cardigans, white ankle socks and sandals. The boys, too, are dressed in virtually identical outfits: white shirts, jumpers, grey shorts, grey socks and black shoes. I am the exception and stand at the end of the row in a jacket and bow tie. I suppose even at such a young age I looked, and must have felt, different.

The most indelible impression of my early childhood was when I started school. Broom Valley Infant School appeared to a small boy of five as a vast, cold and frightening castle of a building with its huge, square, metal-framed windows and endless echoing corridors, shiny green tiles, hard wooden floors and the oppressive smell of stale cabbage and floor polish. The very doors at the entrance looked gargantuan and everything beyond seemed ten times bigger than normal. There was an asphalt playground full of the

Imagination is more important than knowledge. Knowledge is

disconcerting animal din of children who were occupied in manic activity — running, skipping, leaping, jumping, chasing, screaming, shouting, which is still to be heard in primary schools up and down the country today when a large group of children are let loose. Outside each classroom was a row of neatly spaced hooks and I recall wondering what they were for. Maybe the children were hung on them if they were naughty. It was a daunting place and I didn't like it at all and wanted to leave.

On my first day I screamed and shouted, tugged and writhed as my mother held my small hand firmly in hers. I hated it and wanted to go home and sit at the table in the kitchen and help my mother make gingerbread men and listen to her stories. When I saw my mother head for the door, leaving me in the school entrance, I thought I would be abandoned forever and couldn't be consoled. 'I want to go home!' I cried. 'I want to go home!' But I was made to stay, and Miss Wilkinson, the head teacher, took my hand and led me to the infant classroom where I met a young, slim, smiling teacher standing at the door to greet me.

I spent the whole morning whimpering in a corner, resisting the kind attentions of the teacher, Miss Greenhalgh. At morning playtime I couldn't be coaxed to eat the biscuit or drink the milk on offer, and continued to sniffle and whimper. But by lunchtime I had become intrigued and soon dried my tears. Just before lunch, Miss Greenhalgh opened a large coloured picture book and began to read. I loved books, and the bedtime routine was my mother or father or sister snuggling up with me to read. I knew all the

limited. Imagination encircles the world. — *Albert Einstein*

nursery rhymes and the fairy stories and, although I couldn't read, I knew if a word was changed or a bit missed out and would tell the reader so. When Miss Greenhalgh opened the book on that first morning, I stopped the sniffling and listened. She looked to me like someone out of the pages of a fairy tale: long golden hair like Rapunzel's, large blue eyes like Snow White's and such a gentle voice and lovely smile like The Sleeping Beauty's. When she started reading the story, I was completely captivated.

In the afternoon I was keen to hear the rest of the story but the teacher went through a few basics on how we should behave, about going to the toilet before the lesson, washing our hands, to say 'Please' and 'Thank you', to call her Miss, to raise our hands if we wanted something and not to shout out. I was desperate for her to finish the story but then we were all told to lie down on little canvas beds for a nap.

'When will you finish the story?' I asked glumly when it was nearing home time.

'Tomorrow,' replied Miss Greenhalgh, smiling.

The following morning I wolfed down my breakfast, keen to get back to school and Miss Greenhalgh.

I loved those early years at school. We moulded little clay models, dug in the sand pit, played in the water tray, counted with little coloured beads, sang the nursery rhymes, danced with bare feet in the hall, made models with toilet rolls and cardboard boxes, splashed poster paint on large sheets of grey sugar paper, chanted poems and learnt to read. Most of all I loved

Education is that whole system of human training within and without

the fairy stories read by Miss Greenhalgh, stories which celebrated goodness of heart, compassion, kindness to animals, consideration for the poor, weak and elderly and which abhorred greed, selfishness and cruelty. I recall when the wicked stepmother or the ugly sisters got their comeuppance we children cheered.

John Bassett was also apprehensive as he approached school for the first time:

> That morning my face and neck had been scrubbed so hard by my mother they smarted. My father had taken me to the barber's shop on Saturday to have my thatch of ginger hair cut (short back and sides and a lot off the top) and as I stared in disbelief in the mirror, my head looked like a coconut. I was wearing a clean vest and underpants (in case, as my mother pointed out, I had an accident) and a new knitted grey pullover and short trousers (the ones you grow into) held up by an elastic belt with a snake clasp.
>
> I already had tears in my eyes as my mother and I approached this huge blackened stone building with a tower and turrets, a shiny grey slate roof and windows like shining eyes. Surrounding the playground was a huge black iron gate and tall black iron railings with spikes on the top. Perhaps these were to keep the children in, to stop them running away.
>
> 'Don't leave me,' I whimpered, clutching my mother's hand tightly.
>
> 'Now come on John,' she said gently. 'You have to go to

the school house walls, which moulds and develops men. — W E B Du Bois school. You're a big boy now.'

At that moment, shaking with fear, I knew I didn't want to be a big boy. I wanted to stay small forever.

That first morning can be upsetting, particularly if the teacher is not as warm and welcoming as my Miss Greenhalgh. Here's Mrs Elizabeth Mary Atkinson's account which describes her first day at school in 1912:

We had to line up in the playground, hands by our sides, and stand up straight. We were told not to speak but to listen. We were wide-eyed and frightened as the teacher, Miss Bull, a severe-faced woman with her steely-grey hair scraped back savagely on her scalp and into a tiny bun, glittery gimlet eyes and the look of a Gorgon, examined us over the top of steel-framed spectacles as if we were strange specimens in a museum case.

She was like the wicked witch in the fairy tale my mother had read to me. I was so terrified of this ferocious-looking figure in black that I wet my knickers. In the classroom, Miss Bull tut-tutted and shook her head. I was told to remove the knickers and place them on the stove to dry. The room was soon filled with the most noxious smell of which the teacher seemed oblivious but my classmates were not. The other children giggled until Miss Bull whacked her desk with a ruler and bellowed for everyone to be quiet. At playtime two boys in the class shouted, 'Lizzie smelly

She got on with her education. In her opinion,

knickers! Lizzie smelly knickers!' I sat on the low wall and cried and prayed for the time I could leave this horrid place. Later, at home, when I told my mother what had happened her face became flushed with anger. The next morning she came with me to the school, pushed open the black iron gate and marched across the playground with me in tow. She cornered Miss Bull in the classroom and, stabbing a finger in her face, warned her that if she ever did such a cruel thing again she would wring her ugly, wrinkled neck. 'Miss Bull looked so scared,' my mother told my father that evening, 'that it's a wonder *she* didn't wet her knickers.'

Eleanor Rushton's daughter Maisie was quite happy to go to school on the first morning but on the way home after one day looked sad. When asked why she looked so down-in-the-mouth the little girl shook her head and remarked to her mother, 'I don't think my teacher is very good, Mummy. I thought she was going to teach me to read today but I still can't do it.'

On my fifth birthday, I started at the infant school. My mother scrubbed me and I was dressed in my Sunday best. I was delivered to the teacher, Miss Roberts, who stood outside her classroom. We were told to line up and be quiet. We filed into the room and were told where to sit at the small desks facing the front, a boy next to a girl. The boy next to me kept sniffing. Either

school kept on trying to interfere with it. — Terry Pratchett

he was crying or had a cold but whatever it was it irritated me.
The teacher wrote the alphabet on the blackboard and pointed to
each letter, which we had to repeat. During the morning we were
given a small bottle of milk with a straw. It was warm and I
disliked it but we had to drink it all up. In the afternoon Miss
Roberts read a story and then we all climbed on to canvas beds
for our afternoon nap.

Bernice Ashton

My own children never suffered the trauma that I experienced when I
started at the Broom Valley Infant school. Our eldest, Richard, was up early,
dressed and ready, and he skipped to school on his first morning.

'You can go now,' he told my wife when they arrived at the path leading
to the school. Then he raced across the playground to join the other children, leaving his mother crying at the school gates.

After his first day at school my second son Matthew was asked what he
had liked.

'The school dinners were really good,' he said.

Paul Jackson was not as impressed with his school dinners:

On starting primary school I stayed for dinners, even though
we lived only a couple of hundred yards away, as my parents both
worked in local mills. There was no canteen at the school so all

the pupils marched down the road to a room beneath the local chapel. We sat at large make-shift tables, and were served up mainly stewed meat, partly-mashed potatoes and boiled cabbage — apart from Friday fish — followed by either rice pudding, sago (yuk) or everyone's favourite, Manchester tart.

Unusually for a youngster in the late 1950s, I was vegetarian, not that I had any strong beliefs about animal welfare, but because I found great difficulty in eating meat, and strong fish brought me out in a rash. I'd always been like that, and I'm still vegetarian today. At school dinners I would either just leave the meat or fish or swap it for a neighbour's vegetables — generally there were plenty of takers.

However, one day a particularly unsympathetic dinner lady decided she was not putting up with this fussy little urchin and tried to force me to eat the meat. I was obviously some kind of weirdo or an ungrateful so-and-so in her eyes. I could not eat it and as she continued trying to force food down me I threw a tantrum, spat out the meat and charged from the building. I don't know whether anyone came after me. I ran home, broke a window so I could undo the latch, and sat cowering and tearful behind a chair.

The inquest began when Mam arrived home from work, but I don't remember being rebuked, and consequently I never had dinners at primary school again. I went to Gran's house.

the ability to help others learn. — Ruth Beechick

When I started at primary school at seven years of age, my teacher was Mr Rushton. He was a great bear of man with a huge pepper-and-salt beard and large round eyes. I remember his fingers. Like sausages they were. Two of them were missing. My father said he lost them in the war and that he was a very brave man and had been a prisoner. On the first morning we were scared of this huge man but we soon learned to like him for he was a gentle soul and a good teacher who told us stories, read us poems and sang in assembly in a deep growl of a voice.

Linda Wilson

CLASSROOM CREATURES

Mrs Price isn't nice,
Her tiger eyes they burn like ice.
Mr Ryan, hard as iron,
Stalks the classroom like a lion.
Mrs Drew, little shrew,
Very nervous, very new.
Mr Ash, walrus tash,
Brings us all out in a rash.
Dr Gee, can barely see,
A little furry mole is he.

Mrs Page, in a rage,
Like an elephant in a cage.
Mrs Brass, silly ass,
Plays the fool in every class.
Albert Baker, the caretaker,
Dangerous as an alligator.
But Mrs Meacher, our head
  teacher,
Is a most delightful creature.

Everything I need to know ... I learned in kindergarten. — Robert Fulghum

Arnold Greenwood has some unpleasant memories of his first day at grammar school:

I was so excited at the prospect of going to the grammar school. There were only two boys in my primary school class who got through the 11-plus, myself and Derek Rodgers. When the results came out, Mr Mangham, the headmaster of our junior school, called us both to his room after assembly, congratulated us, told us not to be too cock-sure and that we were very lucky to be attending the grammar school which he had attended.

On the first day at the grammar, in my new blazer with the fancy badge and carrying my new satchel, I called for Derek and we walked up the long drive to what looked like a castle. The grammar school was of gaunt black stone with turrets and long windows, and all around us were these big boys who laughed and jeered as we clustered nervously with the other first years. In the assembly that morning the new boys sat at the front of the hall. Stern-faced teachers in black gowns stood down the side. There was a sort of expectant silence. On to the stage strode a tall, hooked-nosed man, also in a black gown. I leaned over to Derek and whispered in his ear, 'That must be the headmaster.'

The figure on the stage stared at me with piercing eyes, then gestured for me with a long thin finger to come out to the front. I climbed up the steps to the stage wondering what he wanted and

Education is a progressive discovery of our own ignorance. — Will Durant

The authority of those who teach is often an obstacle

approached him. He drew back his his hand and slapped me hard across the face, so hard I lost my balance and fell.

'You do not speak, boy, when I am on the stage!' he thundered. 'Do you understand?'

I tried to stem back the tears. All eyes in the hall were upon me. I felt desolate.

'Do you understand?' he repeated. I got to my feet and nodded but could not speak. 'Resume your seat.'

How I hated that horrible man. All through my school days at the grammar I remembered that first morning and my humiliation. When the O-Level results came out, I arrived at school to see how I had done. We had been told to wear our school uniform but I wore denim jeans and a polo neck jumper. I had done really well in my exams, with distinctions in seven of the nine subjects. On my way out the headmaster stopped me.

'Why are you not in uniform?' he demanded.

I had wanted to say this for five years. 'I didn't feel like it.'

'Sir!' he thundered.

'I said I didn't feel like it,' I repeated. My heart was thumping away in my chest but I had waited for this moment.

'What!' he roared. He was clearly disconcerted by what he considered to be my insolence.

I was bigger than he was now, for he was a little man, and I

---

to those who want to learn. — Marcus Tullius Cicero

knew he would not dare hit me. He could bully the little boys but wouldn't try it on with me. I reckon if he had have hit me I would have hit him back. I had nothing to lose. Red in the face and with a trembling voice he told me he would see me first thing when I returned to school in the sixth form.

'You won't,' I replied, 'I'm doing my A-Levels elsewhere.'

And with that, I sauntered out of the school leaving him, I guess, open-mouthed behind me.

Bernard Jenkins has a happier memory of his first week at secondary school:
It was expected by my parents (and I guess by my primary school teacher as well because I was on the top table) that I would pass the eleven plus exam. I didn't, and attended the local secondary modern school: an ugly, featureless, red brick square of a building smack in the middle of the town. On the first morning the first years were divided into three ability groups: A, B and C. I was put in 1B, the middle group. When I got home that afternoon and told my mother she was not pleased at all.

'We'll see about that,' she said.

The following afternoon a prefect came to collect me. He told my teacher, Mr Siddons, that the headmaster wished to see me. On the way down the corridor the prefect asked me what I had done.

It is the mark of an educated mind to be able to

'Nothing,' I replied.

'You don't get to see the "Beaky" (the headmaster's nickname) unless you're getting the stick,' he told me casually.

The headmaster, a tall thin man with silver hair parted down the side, had a huge Roman nose. He sat behind his desk. I was made to stand in front him. 'Your mother has been to see me this morning,' he told me. I remember that he drummed his fingers on the desk top. 'She is of the opinion that you are capable of coping in the A stream. What do you think?'

'I think I could sir,' I managed to say.

'Really.' He leaned back in his chair. 'You think you are up to it, do you?'

'I think I could, Sir,' I repeated.

'We will try you for a couple of weeks in the A stream and see how well you get on. Tell Mr Siddons you are moving into Mr Atkinson's class.' He rubbed his huge nose. 'Work hard, try your best and don't let me or your mother down.'

I held my own in the top class and stayed there.

I have a clear memory of when I started secondary school. There is a photo of me that my mother kept on the sideboard (which we called the 'buffet' for some odd reason) at the age of eleven, posing awkwardly in the back garden in my new black blazer (a good size too big) with large shield-shaped badge on the breast pocket, long grey shorts (obligatory for first and second year pupils), held in place with a striped elastic belt with a snake clasp, knee-length grey socks pulled up tight to the bottom of the knees and anchored there with elastic garters, grey jumper, white shirt, striped tie and polished black shoes.

My ears stick out like jug handles because I had a particularly vicious 'short back and sides' haircut the Saturday before at 'Slasher' Simcox, the demon barber of Rotherham. A new satchel is over my shoulder. I don't look all that excited on my first day at secondary school. I was terrified to be honest. I had heard all the rumours at my junior school as to what happens to new boys and had spent a fitful night thinking about them.

The older boys would wait at the gates shouting and jeering and getting ready to pull your hair, punch you in the stomach, clip you round the ear, steal your dinner money and flush your head down the toilet bowl — lambs to the slaughter. It was a tradition to get the 'first years'. My mother told me such stories were nonsense and if anyone did start to pick on me I should tell her and she would be up to school like lightning. I am afraid I was not altogether reassured.

On that first dread-filled morning I arrived nervously with my friends at the tall wrought iron gates of a huge redbrick building with greasy grey slate roof and high square windows. To a small eleven-year-old it was a massive, towering, frightening edifice resembling a prison or the workhouse I had seen in the film *Oliver Twist*.

In school, you're taught a lesson and then given a test. In life,

Of course, there were no gangs of vicious-looking youths lying in wait to pounce on us, but just groups of boys dressed identically in black blazers with the red badge, some clearly new like myself and looking lost and anxious. The older pupils talked in groups and ignored the younger ones. In the midst of the crowd stood a teacher — a small, barrel-bodied, balding man with little fluffy outcrops around his ears.

With hands on hips he stood in the middle of the playground watching as we trooped though the gates. He was wearing plimsolls and instead of a belt he had a piece of string fastened around the top of his trousers. He looked like a character from Dickens. I learnt later that this was the much-feared Mr Theodore Firth.

Young Tommy was back at home after only two hours of his first day at primary school.

'What's the matter?' asked his mother in concern. 'Why have you returned home so early?'

'Well, I can't read and I can't write,' huffed Tommy, 'and they won't let me talk, so what's the use?'

A five-year-old Dales child, when questioned by his mother how his first day of school had gone, replied with a sigh, 'Well, they din't teach me owt an' I've gorra gu back again tomorra.'

you're given a test that teaches you a lesson. — Tom Bodett

To his mother from Simon, aged 7,
first week at Dour House
Preparatory School, 1950:

TAKE ME HOME!
Oh, mother dear, I hate it here,
Oh, please don't make me stay.
My room is cold, my bed is hard,
And I cry most every day.
Everyone's unfriendly
And I'm feeling so alone.
Oh, mother dear, I hate it here.
Oh, please may I come home?

Now Simon dear, it's mother here,
I've just received your letter.
I'm sure in time you'll settle in
And things will get much better.
I can tell that you're unhappy,
And it's not that I don't care,
But Simon dear, it's best you stay,
You'll get to like it there.

To Simon from his mother, aged 77,
first week at Grimsdale Care
Home, 1999:

TAKE ME HOME!
Oh, Simon dear, I hate it here,
Oh, please don't make me stay.
My room is cold, my bed is hard,
And I cry most every day.
Everyone's unfriendly
And I'm feeling so alone.
Oh, Simon dear, I hate it here.
Oh, please may I come home?

Now mother dear, it's Simon here,
I've just received your letter.
I'm sure in time you'll settle in
And things will get much better.
I can tell that you're unhappy
And it's not that I don't care,
But mother dear, it's best you stay,
You'll get to like it there.

An investment in knowledge pays the best interest. — *Benjamin Franklin*

Chapter Three

PLEASE, SIR!

REMEMBERING MR FIRTH

So –
You are curious to know
What sort of man he was,
What kind of teacher?
Some, I guess, would say that he was unpredictable and loud,
Heavy-handed, hard-headed, proud,
A fiery figure with his froth of wild white hair
And bright, all-seeing eyes,
That he talked too much
And listened too little.

Well –
I'll tell you.
He was a teacher
Who lifted history from the dusty page,

He is either dead or teaching school. — Latin proverb

Re-fought battles on a chalky wooden board.
A storyteller who painted pictures of the past in vivid colour,
An enthusiast who, with bursts of energy
And eyes gleaming with a quick impassioned fire,
Resurrected shadowy characters of a bygone age:
Fabled kings and tragic queens, pale-faced martyrs and holy monks,
Princes and peasants, tyrants and warriors.
He brought history to life.

I recall –
One cold November day,
In a hushed classroom
When he told the story of the sorrowful Scottish queen
Who climbed the scaffold stiffly,
Clad in a gown the colour of dried blood
To meet her fate at Fotheringhay,
And I felt that I was there.

So –
You are curious to know
What sort of man he was,
What kind of teacher?
He was the best.

Schoolmasters: the same persons telling the same people the same

Thomas Love Peacock in Gryll Grange *writes:*
> If all the nonsense which had been talked on all other subjects were thrown onto one scale and all that has been talked on the subject of education alone were thrown into the other, I think the latter would preponderate.

The great majority of people have been through the school system and therefore feel that they have something to say about education — and are not afraid of saying it. They might think twice about challenging a doctor's diagnosis or disagreeing with their solicitor, telling the electrician how to rewire the house or the plumber the best way to mend a leak but when it comes to teachers they are educationalists.

Teachers, it has to be said, are not that popular in the public consciousness. The newspapers invariably carry articles, editorials and letters about the poor state of our education system and the ineffectiveness of our teachers. 'Let teachers take the lessons — and the blame', writes Janet Daley in the *Daily Telegraph.* 'Those who can't, teach …', writes Susan Elkin in the *Daily Mail.* A glance through a week's papers show these two journalists are not alone in their attack on the teaching profession — as these headlines show:

'We have to improve the way we teach religion in schools'
'Better education will improve the economy'
'Lack of creativity lamented in dour schools'
'Teachers becoming the worst cheaters in school exams'

---

things about the same things. — A quotation from Ancient Greece

'Ex-soldiers to be brought into schools to help give pupils discipline'
'How right they were to take a whack at the teachers'
'150,000 children unable to read and write at 11'
'English school leavers lagging behind entire developed world'
It has ever been the case that teachers have come in for criticism.

> *The bookful blockhead, ignorantly read,*
> *With loads of learned lumber in his head.*
>
> *Alexander Pope*

Perhaps this antipathy to teachers comes from hazily remembered schooldays when 'Sir' or 'Miss' ruled supreme in the classroom and made life uncomfortable and sometimes painful for their pupils. Ideally, what should be said to every child, repeatedly, throughout his or her school life is something like this: 'You are in the process of being indoctrinated. We have not yet evolved a system of education that is not a system of indoctrination.'

Doris Lessing, The Golden Notebook

Pupils have never credited teachers for most of their learning. Bright and dull alike have always relied on rote, reading a wit to pass their exams, motivated by the stick or by the carrot of a

---

God forgive me for having thought it possible that a schoolmaster

desired career ... schools create jobs for school teachers,
no matter what their pupils learn from them.

Ivan Illich

A road safety poster outside a London school stated:
'DRIVE CAREFULLY. DON'T KILL A CHILD.'
Underneath someone had written:
WAIT FOR A TEACHER!

Certainly when I asked friends and family about their memories of school
and their teachers some were less than complimentary:

I had a particularly unpleasant form master who would make
sarcastic comments, flew into rages, was too handy with a slipper
and had the habit of ripping up pages out of our exercise books if
our writing was untidy. I think he was quite an unhappy man and
didn't like children. He was a stickler for neatness and checked the
contents of our desks at regular intervals to make sure everything
was orderly.

He was obsessive about the text books we used, scrutinising
them at various times to ensure that there were no scribbles in
the margins or pages with turned-down corners. He was forever
reminding us that they were expensive and must be taken great
care of. After the last lesson with him just before we sat our

could be out and out a rational being. — Sir Walter Scott

O-Levels, we had to hand in these text books, and were told to stack them neatly on his desk. Over lunchtime several of us took our text books to the woodwork room and cut them in half with a fret saw. Then we placed them in the middle of the pile of books on his desk. We never did witness his reaction but imagined it with great pleasure.

Philip Graves

'When a teacher calls a boy by his entire name, it means trouble,' Mark Twain once said. At secondary school the teachers all called us just by our last names which I really didn't like. They never called the girls by their second names. One particular teacher, Mr Banister, would roll the 'r' in my name to make it sound like an insult. 'Prrrraaaat!' he would shout. Years later I was in town when I met my former teacher.

'It's Pratt isn't it?' he said.

'Yes,' I replied. 'And you're Banister.'

Michael Pratt

The sports mistress, Miss Palmer, was an unpleasant woman who only bothered with those girls who were good at games and PE and who were in the school teams. I was tall, gangly, uncoordinated and clumsy, and invariably consigned with other

---

I have always had a certain loathing of schoolmasters, feeling them

unfit and ungainly girls to what was known as the 'scrags' — the mediocre group — which was left pretty much to its own devices on the games field. Occasionally, the teacher, dressed in a thick track suit and fleece-lined jacket, would leave the teams she was refereeing and wander over to us to shout.

Those of us in the 'scrags' wore shorts and thin white cotton blouses and in winter we were freezing cold. I hated the icy wind which turned your legs blue, and being shouted at. I remember one moment of great pleasure when, hidden from view in a classroom one lunchtime, I overheard Miss Palmer attempting to argue with the drama teacher.

Both had wanted Irene Baker, who was good at both drama and sports (and pretty much good at everything else), to attend their sessions after school. Irene had to decide whether to attend the rehearsal for the school play or the hockey coaching and she had approached both teachers to sort it out. Mrs Milner, the drama teacher, was a large, loud and intimidating woman who nobody would dare cross. She, of course, won the argument, sending her colleague off with a flea in her ear. How I chuckled to hear Miss Palmer shouted at.

Debbie Saunders

---

to be a corrupt body of creatures on the whole. — Robert Morley

NEW BOY
When we had PE,
The new boy changed in the toilets
Out of sight of all the others.
'Shy, are we?' asked the teacher, smirking
When the boy emerged in grubby shirt and shorts.
'Come along, son, let's have that top off.
You cannot do PE wrapped up like that.'
'Please sir,' pleaded the boy, 'can I keep it on?'
'You heard me!' snapped the teacher.
With downcast eyes, the new boy
Pulled the shirt slowly over his head
And we all saw the dark blue bruises on the thin white arms.

I hated games and PE not just because I was poor at anything physical. I was undersized as a child and very conscious of the way I looked compared with those of my age. The other boys seemed to shoot up at adolescence but I remained small for my age. They used to call me 'pint-size' or 'titch'. It was the showers that upset me the most. The PE master, a big bear of a man with a tracksuit full of coloured badges showing how good he was at sports, made us all strip after the lesson and go in the communal shower. It was then that the other boys had a laugh at my

The only thing I remember learning in the Home Economics

expense. Most were well developed, I was not and they jeered and laughed. I had never felt so vulnerable and unhappy.

Gerard Smith

The careers teacher offered no advice worth taking. It was the steelworks, the pit or the army. If anyone asked if there might be any other kind of work he would direct us to a huge cardboard box crammed with careers literature and say, 'Have a look in there.'

Thomas White

I hated school. At the secondary modern which I attended we were written off. We were the 11-plus failures and on the strength of the examination we were put on the educational scrapheap, destined for the menial jobs in society.

Certainly higher education was not considered an option for us. It was clear to me that the teachers felt it a waste of their time and effort to try and teach us anything academic so we spent long hours doing woodwork and metalwork, gardening and technical drawing.

It was not unusual for the teachers to leave us unattended and untaught for long periods of time. Books were not marked, homework not set and they had little expectation of us. This

lesson was how to starch a tray cloth. — Jennifer Wright

produced in many of us a low self-esteem, a lack of belief in ourselves. I was in work for a couple of years before I realised I was not stupid but had potential.

Barry McCann

I don't remember my schooldays as being a particularly happy time. Some teachers tried to make the lessons interesting but most got us to copy out of text books and they looked as bored as we were. No child should be called a fool or an idiot, stupid or ignorant, and yet I recall teachers using those sorts of words as a matter of course. I shall never forget when one teacher, before handing me back my work, ripped the page out of my book and told me what I had written was rubbish and that I was brainless.

Gerard Basset

The owner of the corner shop arrived at the school to complain tthat children had been stealing sweets. When she questioned some of the pupils who had been in her shop that lunchtime my name came up and I was sent for. Despite protesting my innocence (I might have been a lot of things at school but I was not a thief), I received three strokes of the cane, 'as an example to others not to steal' I was told. I shall never forget the unfairness.

Gary Wilson

Education makes people easy to lead but difficult to drive;

In the little world in which children have their existence
whosoever brings them up, there is nothing so finely perceived
and so finely felt as injustice. It may be only small injustice that
the child can be exposed to; but the child is small, and its world
is small, and its rocking-horse stands as many hands high,
according to scale, as a big-boned Irish hunter.

Charles Dickens in Great Expectations

Then, the whining schoolboy with his satchel / And shining
morning face, creeping like snail / Unwillingly to school …

William Shakespeare, As You Like It

The school I attended did little when it came to tackling
bullying. I think the masters thought it was all a part of growing
up. If you did tell a master he would say, 'Just ignore it', or 'Don't
tell tales'. I guess they thought that it would toughen us up and
prepare us for the harsh world that lay ahead. Some children take
delight in making others unhappy, calling them names, picking on
them in the yard. One boy in particular was nasty. His party piece
was spitting from a distance, usually at the younger boys who
were too frightened to do anything. I was one of those. It is a fact
that bullies forget. Those who have been bullied never do.

George Hutchinson

---

easy to govern, but impossible to enslave. — Lord Brougham

LETTER TO A BULLY
Dear Martin,
I saw your name in the paper
The other day.
I thought I'd write.
You probably won't remember me
But I remember you.

I remember your cold blue eyes
And nasty smile,
And how you mouthed: 'You're dead!'
Across the classroom
When the teacher looked the other way.

I remember my cut lip
And bloody nose,
And how I rubbed by bruised shins
On the way home,
When you had run off laughing.

I remember the ache and hurt
And fear inside,
And how I dreaded end of school,

For who will be taught, if he be not moved with

With you in wait outside
To push me up against the wall.

Yes, I saw your name in the paper
The other day,
And thought I'd write.
As I said you probably won't remember me
But, oh, how I remember you.

At secondary school we had a history teacher who, to a young teenager, already appeared to be part of ancient history himself: craggy-faced, grey-haired and always wearing a shiny, ill-fitting, out-of-fashion suit. He was eccentric, too. He seemed to have eyes in the back of his head, and would accuse individual pupils behind him of talking or not paying attention, while he chalked copious notes on the blackboard.

We would have to copy his scrawl into our books then learn the words parrot-fashion as homework. The next lesson would then see us regurgitate the words as if in an exam. No one dared mess about during his lessons for fear of having the board duster hurled at them.

His cleaning of the blackboard was legendary. He and the first row of pupils would be covered in white chalk dust as he

a desire to be taught? — Sir Philip Sidney

frantically wiped away his notes — even if the slower writers hadn't yet finished copying them down — to refill the board with his words of wisdom. One day, he wiped the board so vigorously the wooden duster flew out of his hand and through an open window. One particular boy, who for some reason usually bore the brunt of his ire, was yelled at as though it was his fault and told to retrieve the errant duster.

Paul Jackson

A friend, talking to me about his schooldays and the tougher discipline in schools, recalled his former teacher, in almost affectionate terms, who would throw a board rubber at anyone in the class not paying attention. The pupils became adept at dodging the missile. 'It never did us any harm,' my friend told me. Had the board rubber found its target and hit a pupil in the eye it would indeed have done harm.

Ernest Thompson

Some of us have happier memories and my education proved a useful source of quaint, amusing, poignant and nostalgic material which I have drawn on in my books. Some writers, describing their schooldays, dwell on their unhappiness at the hands of bullies and the cruelty at the hands of teachers. They speak of chalk thrown across the classroom, trouser bottoms

Free the child's potential, and you will transform

smoking after a vicious caning, sarcastic, incompetent and sometimes sadistic teachers. Well, my schooldays were very different and I remember my teachers with great affection and gratitude.

Mr Schofield was in charge of geography. He was a sensitive, tolerant man, always willing to listen but not a soft touch. He was never too preoccupied to talk informally to the pupils at break times or too impatient to go over an explanation again if we were unsure. He was a natural teacher who enjoyed teaching, handled dissenting voices with humour and always made us feel valued. Those of us who have been teachers know only too well how daunting it can be to stand in front of a group of large, volatile adolescents, not accustomed to sitting still and listening, and attempt to engage their attention and get them to do as they are told. It is important to appear strong and fearless even if it is an act.

Many years later, Mr Schofield, then in his eighties, came to hear me when I appeared on stage at the Strode Theatre in Street. I sat in the bar after my performance with his wife and family and we reminisced. He reminded me of the time when he joined in with the laughter when a boy by the name of Paul Watson asked about a particular rock that his father had sent into school to be identified. It had traces of a coloured metal in it.

'Do you know what it is, Sir?' asked the pupil.

The bright spark of the class, quick as a flash, shouted out, 'It's sedimentary, my dear Watson!'

Ken Pike taught me for my O-Levels in English Language and English

him into the world. — Maria Montessori (1870–1952)

Literature. He was an inspirational teacher who infected me with a love of language and an appreciation of literature. He spoke with wonderful conviction and developed in me a passion for the written word.

As an inspector I often thought that if the material is appropriate to the age and maturity of the students, and if the teacher manages to interest and challenge the students, that they possess some sensitivity, understanding and have a sense of humour, then there would be far fewer discipline problems in schools. It is often when the lessons are dull and the teacher lacklustre that poor discipline emerges. Mr Pike had a great sense of humour. It is of inestimable importance that teachers do have a sense of humour: indeed, a sense of fun.

Mr Theodore Firth (Theo) was a very different sort of teacher from the other members of staff. He was a stout, red-cheeked man with tufts of sandy-coloured hair at the side of an otherwise bald head and a roar like a lion and a stare like the sweep of a scythe. He was the archetypal Yorkshire-man: bullish, plain-speaking, lacking in sophistication, a no-nonsense sort of man who could put the very fear of God into his pupils. There was no pacing up and down the classroom for him, no sitting on the end of the desk and, above all, no noise. He would stand like some great Eastern statue, legs apart, arms folded over his barrel chest, jaw jutting out, surveying the neat lines of desks which faced the front of his classroom.

Some would say that there is no room in education for teachers such as Mr Firth, those unusual individuals who are out of the ordinary,

Far too many children have learning difficulties, induced by the fact

idiosyncratic, who don't always follow the various directives. In my view they are wrong. Such teachers frequently have a greater impact than the more conventional teachers and are often remembered years later when the 'ordinary' teachers have been long forgotten. Mr Firth was strict but he was scrupulously fair, totally committed but rather unpredictable and, provided you worked hard and were well-behaved, he posed no problem. He insisted on every pupil's undivided attention, neat and accurate writing and work completed on time. In answer to his questions he expected the right hand of the pupil to be raised straight as a die and for the pupil to answer clearly and confidently.

I well recall his description of the Battle of Culloden; the ill-equipped and bedraggled clansmen were dragged from their homes in feudal observance to their chieftains to follow Bonnie Prince Charlie. Armed with only claymores and farming implements, they met the long ranks of heavily-armed, disciplined English redcoats who knocked them over like ninepins. Several pupils were asked to come out to the front of the class with rulers to represent the bayonets of the English troops and claymores of the Scottish. Theo demonstrated that each English soldier had been instructed to bayonet the opponent to his right who would be lifting his sword arm and thus exposing his body. In my mind I saw and heard the vivid picture of the English army in crimson jackets marching in strict order, bayonets fixed, the periwigged officers on white horses, the skirling of the Highland pipes and the wild rush of the tartan clad clansmen.

---

that their teachers have teaching difficulties. — Keith Waterhouse

I studied for my A-Level English in Oakwood Girls' High School in Rotherham and it was there that I met the teacher who made a profound impression upon me. Miss Mary Wainwright was a diminutive, softly-spoken woman dressed in a pristine white blouse with lace collar, buttoned up at the neck with small pearl buttons. She was swathed in a long, pleated tweed skirt, dark brown stockings and small leather brogues. The delicate embroidered handkerchief that she secreted up her sleeve would be occasionally plucked out to dab her mouth. Save for the large cameo brooch placed at her throat, she wore no jewellery and there was no vestige of make-up. She lined up her new students, a motley group of spotty, lanky boys, and peered up at us. 'I've never taught boys,' she said, and then after a long pause and with a twinkle in her dark eyes she added, 'but I've heard of them.'

We studied two of Shakespeare's greatest plays — *Richard II* and *Hamlet*, the longest and most tedious of Chaucer's *Canterbury Tales*, *The Knight's Tale* and *The Prologue*, *The Grapes of Wrath* by John Steinbeck, *Joseph Andrews* by the eighteenth-century novelist Henry Fielding and the poetry of John Keats. I was pleased to see that Thomas Hardy's tragic tale, *The Mayor of Casterbridge*, was on the syllabus but disappointed that D H Lawrence and Charles Dickens were not.

As soon as Miss Wainwright opened the book and started to read I was in a world I loved and with which I felt familiar. Occasionally she would stop, make a comment and smile with a curious wistfulness, as if there was something she recalled fondly from a distant past.

Poor is the pupil who does not surpass

In the Handbook for Teachers *published in 1918 is an interesting paragraph:*
The teacher need not let the sense of his responsibility depress him or make him afraid to be his natural self in school. Children are instinctively attracted by sincerity and cheerfulness; and the greatest teachers have been thoroughly human in their weaknesses as well as in their strength.

To admit his or her ignorance and error is not a sign of weakness in a teacher. My former art teacher Mr Cooper (Harry) is a case in point. Alec, my brother, was his star pupil and went on to art school and a very successful career in painting and music. I remember once at the art club after school, when I was in the first year, Mr Cooper looked at my pathetic effort — a clumsy drawing of a green wine bottle and bowl of fruit — with a critical eye, a cigarette dangling from his lips. 'I think the skill with the paintbrush stopped with your brother,' he remarked sadly.

When he had moved on to look at John Pacey's work, I screwed up my painting, threw it in the bin and left the room, angry tears stinging my eyes. The next morning a school prefect came to fetch me at registration. I was to report to Mr Cooper. I knew I would be in trouble for storming out of the room and not clearing up all the paints and brushes I had used. I waited outside the art room, rehearsing in my head what I would say to him. The door opened and the teacher emerged.

'I am sorry for what I said yesterday,' Mr Cooper said quietly and rather

his master. — Leonardo da Vinci

shame-facedly. 'I was in the wrong to compare you with your brother. I thought what a foolish thing it was to say as soon as I had said it and I meant to have a word with you at the end of the session but you went home. I can quite understand why you left. Anyway, I'm sorry. I hope you will accept my apology.'

'Yes Sir,' I said. I could feel my heart thumping in my chest — a teacher apologising to a pupil was unheard of.

'Thank you,' he said and held out his hand for me to shake.

'It was pretty poor though, Sir, wasn't it? I asked him.

'I'm afraid it was,' he replied, smiling.

A teacher who admits to his mistakes and is prepared to apologise to a pupil gains infinitely more respect than one who is never in the wrong and sees the words 'I'm sorry' as a weakness. Mr Cooper went up greatly in my estimation that day. What incredible good fortune it was for me to have had these remarkable teachers.

Like me, the following people had fond memories of their time in school:

I was sent to see Mr Price, the deputy head teacher, for coming late to school yet again. I just never seemed to get to school on time and after repeated warnings and the threat of the cane, I still didn't manage to arrive before the bell. Over the weeks I had shot up and my blazer was too small and my flannel trousers too tight. When I bent over and presented my bottom for the cane the trousers split. Mr Price, who was a decent sort of chap, burst out laughing and told me to return to class. I never did get the cane.

Malcolm Wright

Sister Protase was something of a legend at the convent high school which I attended. She was a warm, good-humoured and enthusiastic teacher and we loved her lessons. One story about her was when she was travelling by steam train. She found the carriage was occupied by several businessmen. There was only one vacant seat. Two of them stood and made room for her. Recognising the man sitting opposite her as a parent of a child in the school where she taught, she leaned forward and smiling said, 'I have an idea you are the father of one of my children.'

Geraldine O'Connor

A most earnest and amiable monk at the school where I was taught used to say that the nearest our finite minds could ever approach to an understanding of heaven was to imagine a state of perpetual sexual intercourse. At that early age we accepted his teaching, but it is important to remember that in those days none of us had ever experienced what he was talking about any more than he had.

Auberon Waugh

it, unless it agrees with your own reason and your own common sense. — Buddha

Mrs Faraday, the French teacher, had a bowl of plastic fruit on her desk. She would hold up an apple and ask, 'Que'est-ce que c'est?' and we were supposed to shout back, 'C'est une pomme.' Then she'd pick up a pear and ask, 'Qu'est-ce que c'est?' and we'd shout back, 'C'est une poire.' Once, she held up a plastic banana. 'Qu'est-ce que c'est?' she asked but caught sight of a boy talking at the back of the classroom. She let fly with the plastic banana. It flew straight through the air like a missile, hit him straight between eyes, ricocheted off his forehead and flew back to her like a boomerang. She put up her hand and caught it. All the class jumped to their feet and gave her a standing ovation.

Frances Davies

The field at the secondary modern school which I attended abutted the playing fields of the grammar school. We had this one scrubby field; they had a rugger pitch, two football pitches and a cricket square. We felt badly done to and I suppose there was a fair bit of resentment on our side. Skirmishes broke out between us and the 'grammar school nobs' when we were on our way to school. I guess the teachers at our school must have felt some resentment too.

On one occasion, my friend Tony Moss grabbed the cap of a grammar school lad and threw it into the canal. He was identified

A wise man is one who finally realises that there are some

and the headmaster of the grammar must have contacted our headmaster and asked him to discipline the culprit. We all expected Tony to get the cane but he emerged from the headmaster's room smiling and said, 'He just told me not to do it again.'

Norman Ford

Each year at the Catholic grammar school which I attended some of the boys went on a 'retreat'. We would spend a weekend at a Catholic boarding school in Yorkshire and, between listening to various priests give talks and lead discussions, we would play football and make use of the swimming pool which were great incentives for us to go.

We would sleep overnight in the dormitories. On the Saturday night I couldn't sleep. The bed was old and had broken springs, it was too hot, and the other boys snored. At about midnight, when the moon was shining through the window, I saw the shape of a hooded figure with outstretched arms standing by the wall at the end of the room. I was terrified. It didn't move but remained there. I buried my head under the bedclothes and prayed it would go away.

The next morning, when a bright sun lit up the room, I saw what it was which produced the shape: the statue of a benevolent looking Jesus with welcoming arms which stood on a table. It had been projected and enlarged in the moonlight. Years later when I

questions one can ask which may have no answers. — Anon

studied *Macbeth* for O-Level the lines in Act 2 had a particular
(although perhaps not very apposite) resonance for me:
  … *'tis the eye of childhood*
  That fears a painted devil.

Leonard Morris

I honestly cannot fault my teachers. Under sometimes difficult
circumstances they managed to be dedicated and good-
humoured and were always there if I needed help. They gave me
a love of learning. You can't say better than that.

Martin Bowler

Teachers are our heroes. We believe that they should be
everyone's heroes. Anyone who has watched a teacher begin a
day facing a group of kids who would rather be anywhere else in
the world than sitting in that classroom learning something called
geometry that they couldn't care less about, understands only too
well what a frustrating, thankless, enervating task these mortal
men and women face so much of their working lives. In return
they feel unappreciated, disrespected, the focus of twisted media
attacks, caught in an almost war-like situation not of their making.

The Ontario Royal Commission on Learning, 1994

Whoever educates a child undertakes the most

We all have a favourite teacher and Miss Bronson was mine. Gentle, kindly, quietly spoken, she brought history to life. When our exam results came out and we had all passed history, she cried.

Marlene Johnson

Most teachers have some happy memories of when they were in the classroom. Here are a few reminiscences:

The vicar had been asked to take the school assembly. As he walked to the front of the hall he overheard a boy mutter, 'Oh God! It's him!'

'No,' the cleric told the boy. 'Just a pal of his.'

Annette Jones

When I was a newly qualified teacher I saw a boy dropping a sweet paper in the library. I was determined to exert my discipline and teach him a lesson and told him to report to me after school. Before the bell for the end of school, I emptied the remains of two waste paper baskets all over the library floor and added some torn-up paper and screwed-up tissues for good measure.

I explained to the caretaker, who was watching, that it was to teach a pupil a lesson in not dropping litter and that he would be returning at the end of school to pick everything up. At four o'clock the miscreant never arrived. The caretaker, hands on his

important duty of society. — Samuel Wilberforce

hips, stood at the library door and announced, 'Well I'm not cleaning all this bloody lot up. You dropped it, you pick it up.' I chuckled to myself as I attacked the litter.

Martin Barber

I was returning from the theatre with my wife one Saturday night. The town centre was unusually quiet and as we turned down a dark and deserted street leading to the car park a group of hooded boys walked towards us. One of them, a tall and rather scary-looking individual, looked in my direction and then crossed the road. His companions followed. My heart beat in my chest and I took a deep breath, expecting the worst.

'Hello Mr Foster,' said the boy cheerfully. 'Do you remember me? You used to teach me woodwork.' He turned to his mates. 'He were a good teacher was Mr Foster.'

Norman Foster

On sports' day at the special school where I worked, the children set off for the first race. Halfway down the track the girl who was leading the runners fell. The boy behind her immediately stopped, helped her to her feet and putting his arm around her, shepherded her from the field.

Alison Riley

Education: a succession of eye-openers each involving the

repudiation of some previously held belief. — George Bernard Shaw

The builders were resurfacing the flat roof above my classroom one hot summer afternoon and all the windows were open. The air was blue with the builders' choice language, which could clearly be heard by the children who sat before me. My class could see that I was not best pleased. I told them to get on with their work and that I would be back in a minute. As I headed for the door one of the pupils poked his head out of the open window and shouted up at the builders, 'Oi! You lot up there! Our teacher's getting you done.'

Steph Morgan

I attended the hospital for some tests and was asked to wait by the nurse in a small room. The doctor who arrived to see me I recognised as one of my former pupils.

'Hello, Mr Thompson,' she said.

'Oh hello, Amanda,' I replied sheepishly.

'Take off your clothes and I will be with you presently,' she said with a smile.

Andrew Thompson

When I was a college lecturer, I visited a secondary school in the inner city to observe a music student on teaching practice. She was a delightful young woman and clearly related well to the thirteen-year-olds she taught. In one lesson she sat on the edge of her desk

---

No man who worships education has got the best out of education … Without a

and played her guitar. She then asked a girl to come out and place
a hand on the instrument while she strummed the strings.

'Can you feel anything Rosie?' she asked. 'A sort of tingling in
your fingers?' The girl nodded. 'That's a vibration.'

'My mam's got one of those in her drawer at home,' chimed up
a girl on the back row.

T J Murphy

The headmaster of the grammar school where I taught was in
the habit of walking around the premises each morning before the
start of lessons to make sure none of the pupils was late for class.
He arrived at the bike sheds where he discovered two boys in
earnest conversation.

'And pray what is this?' he asked. 'A little *converzatione*?'

'No Sir,' replied one of the boys, patting the saddle on his
bicycle, 'it's a Raleigh Mustang.'

F D

I worked with a teacher colleague who spent much of her time
shouting at the children. I taught in the adjoining classroom which
had an interconnecting door, and each morning I would hear her
bellowing at the children. It not only disturbed my lessons and
annoyed me but I felt sorry for her class. In my experience children

---

gentle contempt for education no man's education is complete. — G K Chesterton

do not like to be constantly shouted at. Who does? I did mention this to my colleague but she informed me loftily that what she did in her classroom was her concern and not mine.

One morning I was reading the poem *The Highwayman* by Alfred Noyes to my eleven-year-olds and the noise from next door was particularly strident — so much so that the children were more interested in hearing the harangue than listening to the poem. I had brought into school an old pistol to illustrate what the highwayman would have used to hold up the coaches. I had had enough of the shouting and, opening the interconnecting door to the classroom, interrupted my colleague's lesson.

'Might I borrow a stick of chalk?' I asked pleasantly.

She stopped shrieking mid-sentence. 'Yes of course,' she said. 'There's a box of chalk on my desk.'

I departed and the shouting resumed. I made a second entrance a moment later. 'Might I trouble you for a coloured stick of chalk?' I asked.

'Yes,' she replied, clearly irritated at being interrupted again.

I left, but a few seconds later I made my final entrance. 'Actually,' I said, pointing the gun, 'I'll have the box.'

Sad to say my colleague did not see the funny side. I was summoned to see the head teacher later that day. He had received a complaint about my behaviour and informed me,

The object of teaching a child is to enable him

with a trace of a smile upon his lips, that it was not at all professional to hold a colleague up at gunpoint.

Simon Brown

A young woman teacher was guiding her class of infants across a busy road when the lights turned to red. An impatient driver asked her sarcastically, 'Don't you know when to stop?'

Smiling she replied, 'Oh, they are not all my children you know.'

C J

I always felt it a privilege to be a teacher. There is no job like it. Every day is different and each year you meet a new set of children, most of whom are keen to learn. I once heard someone say that teachers are not doing the children a favour by teaching them but they are doing us a favour by letting us.

Janice Walker

One lunchtime we were in the staff room when we heard knocking. 'Come in!' someone shouted, but no one came. This was followed by more knocking so someone opened the door. Nobody was there. The knocking continued and still no one came in, so I went out and opened the door of the store cupboard immediately next door. In there stood a small child looking perplexed.

to get along without a teacher. — Elbert Hubbard

'What are you doing in here?' I asked.

'Trying to come out,' he said.

He'd been taken in there to change his wet pants, left to finish off, and someone kindly pulled the door shut.

Diane French

Part of my joy in learning is that it puts me in a position to teach; nothing, however outstanding and however helpful, will give me any pleasure if the knowledge is for my benefit alone. If wisdom were offered me on the one condition that I should keep it shut away and not divulge it to anyone, I should reject it. There is no enjoying the possession of anything valuable unless one has someone to share it with.

Seneca, Letters from a Stoic

Miss Sanderson, the French mistress, was an old and very refined woman who invariably dressed in a pristine white blouse and pleated tweeds. She had her own china mug and ate rich tea biscuits with her coffee at morning break. She smelled of lavender. The mathematics teacher, Mr Drayton, had been cleaning out the old books from his storeroom and came across a dusty tome listing all the old terms for weights and measures, words like 'rod' and 'perch', 'peck' and 'bushel'. He was asking some of the older

There is less flogging in our great schools than formerly — but then less is learned

colleagues in the staff room if they recalled any of the old-fashioned terms.

'For example,' he said to Miss Sanderson, 'did you ever come across a firkin?'

'A firkin what, Mr Drayton?' she asked with a wry smile.

Jack Drake

I was teaching a Year 11 Design Technology group how to draw up plans for their projects. All the boys were equipped with pencils, rulers and drawing instruments.

'Right lads,' I said, 'get out your tools.'

'Is this to be testicular drawing then Sir?' asked the classroom wit.

C J Black

I had written an article for an educational journal about the rise in political correctness in schools. It came about as a result of a lecture I had given after which I was informed by a head teacher that the term 'brainstorm', which I had used to describe the activity when children are encouraged to suggest ideas and words, was inappropriate. 'It could be upsetting,' he told me, 'to those who have brainstorms.' I was told that the correct words I should use were 'thought-shower' or 'cloudburst'.

Another term deemed unacceptable was 'nitty-gritty'. After another talk which I gave I was told that it was a derogatory term for slaves in the early

there; so what the boys get at one end they lose at the other. — Samuel Johnson

Adults laugh up to twenty times a day, whilst young children

1900s, or even worse, a euphemistic term for the practice of forcing intercourse on the female slaves under one's 'ownership'. It is also believed, the
teacher informed me, to be a euphemism for the layer of excrement at the
bottom of a slave ship after a transatlantic crossing. Hence to 'get down to
the nitty-gritty'. I did take the trouble of referring to the *Oxford English Dic-
tionary* and discovered the term is of twentieth-century coinage. Surely,
therefore, the phrase could not relate to the issues described by the
offended teacher.

Anyway, following the publication of this article I received a letter from a
Mrs Goodbody regarding political correctness in schools. Mrs Goodbody (I
was a tad suspicious about the name, I have to admit) related the story of her
visit to Doncaster racecourse with her class of infants with a couple of junior-
aged children to assist. It offered, she felt, a good educational opportunity for
the children to learn about road safety on their walk to the racecourse, see the
horses and do some creative writing when they were back in school.

She went on to tell me she could never do this in the modern politically-
correct climate for she would be accused, no doubt, of encouraging the
children to gamble.

'In any case,' she wrote, 'I wouldn't do it again after the incident.'

I shall let her take up the story …

'We hadn't been at the racecourse long before two or three of the little
boys approached me and asked if they could go to the toilet. I asked Mrs
Smith, my colleague, to look after the rest of the children while I took the

---

laugh as much as three hundred. — Dr Pierce J Howard

children to the portaloos. The first child came out of the toilets after a few seconds and informed me that he 'couldn't go because the thing you do it in is right up on the wall'. I had no option but to go into the toilet, pull down the child's pants and point him at the urinal. I did the same with the next three little boys. The last in line I found to be somewhat taller, heavier and (I couldn't help noticing) well-endowed.

"Are you one of the junior boys?" I asked.

"No, Madam," he replied, "I'm riding Arctic Mist in the three o'clock."'
(There is an old saying that one should never let the truth get in the way of a good story.)

I was greeted in the entrance of the exclusive five-star London hotel by a doorman resplendent in frock coat and top hat. I was there with my wife for a charity luncheon.

'Mr Phinn?' he enquired.

'Yes,' I replied, surprised to be recognised.

'The manager would like to see you in his office, sir, if you would like to follow me.'

I turned to Christine. 'Probably read one of my books.'

'I don't think so sir,' said the doorman. 'The manager is rather angry with you from what I gather.'

'Angry with me?' I repeated. 'Whatever for?'

'I wouldn't know, sir,' he replied.

If you ask what is the goal of education in general, the answer is easy:

In his plush office the manager rose from his large mahogany desk. He was a tall, elegant man of about fifty.

'Mr Phinn,' he said. 'I am glad to have the opportunity of seeing you at last.'

'Do I know you?' I asked.

'Oh yes, you know me.'

'I believe I have upset you in some way,' I said.

'Indeed you have.'

'Perhaps you might tell me what I have done?'

He smiled. 'You see you never believed me when I told you the dog ate my homework.'

'What!' I exclaimed.

'You used to teach me. We had a Jack Russell terrier called Jackie and it chewed up my English homework. You said it was such a far-fetched excuse and made me stay in over lunchtime and think of a more imaginative reason. You didn't believe me.'

'I see,' I said.

'You don't remember me, do you?' he continued.

'No,' I said. 'I'm afraid I don't.'

'Michael Brennan.'

'Michael Brennan,' I sighed. I then recalled the boy I taught some thirty-five-or-so years ago, the quietly-spoken, well-behaved boy who assisted the priest on the altar.

'I was telling the truth.' he said.

it is to make good men and good women act nobly. — Plato

'I'm sorry Michael,' I said. 'Sometimes teachers get it wrong.'

His face broke into a great smile. 'I always enjoyed your lessons,' he told me, 'and today, Mr Phinn, you won't pay for a drink.'

Several years ago, at my first teaching job in Menston, the headmistress, who got absolutely furious with a child, was overheard to say: "If you do that one more time I'll smack your hand with my bottom."

We beat a hasty retreat and collapsed in fits round the corner. I still laugh about that today.

Angela Stringer

TEACHER
There was an old teacher called Blewitt,
Who was clever, and oh how he knew it.
'Pay attention!' he roared.
'The work's on the board.
Take a look and then I'll go through it!'

But, good gracious, you've got to educate him first. You can't expect a boy

Chapter Four

THE INNOCENCE OF CHILDREN

Children are the everlasting new start to life springing up again, joyous and undefiled. I know that my children must make the mistakes that I have made, commit the same sins, be tormented by the same passions, as I know that green shoots pushing up from the earth must ripen and fall back dead onto that same earth, yet this does not take away from the wonder and beauty of children or the spring.

Malcolm Muggeridge, A Life

'There is nothing so affecting,' said the poet Coleridge, 'as the innocence of children.' Even those who do not have children, grandchildren or who have not taught the very young, will know this to be true. For children everything in the world is new and colourful and interesting; they do not know about the things that often divide the adult world — skin colour, race, religion, class, status, money — and unlike some adults they are never

to be vicious till he's been to a good school. — Saki

cynical. They are not afraid of asking questions or saying what they think; they are full of humour (often unconsciously so) and say the most amusing things. There is much truth in the old proverb: 'Here's to the child and all he has to teach us.'

> *What are those blue remembered hills,*
> *What spires, what farms are those?*
> *That is the land of lost content,*
> *I see it shining plain,*
> *The happy highways where I went*
> *And cannot come again.*
>
> *A E Housman,* A Shropshire Lad *(1896)*

Travelling to London by train one cold, overcast, miserable day, I sat at a table with two other passengers. Suddenly, a little head appeared over the seat in front. The four-year-old began to pull faces so I pulled faces back. He giggled. I smiled. His daddy caught sight of his young son and told the child not to pull faces for it would disturb the man in the seat behind. He had not seen me pulling faces. My eyes met those of the child. He could have told his father that that man in the seat behind was making faces at him but he didn't. He gave a small smile as if to say, 'I won't tell.'

Later in the journey he stood in the aisle and announced, 'I can see my daddy's erection in the window.'

We are shut up in schools for ten or fifteen years, and come out at last with a

The little boy's father, red in the face, shot to his feet and told the whole of the carriage. 'He means my reflection.' The effect of this was to fill the carriage with laughter and people started to talk to each other.

'My grandson is forever saying things like that,' said the woman sitting next to me. 'He once said "Grannie, your face needs ironing".'

The man sitting opposite joined the conversation. 'My grandson once asked me who would fetch the fish and chips when I was dead.'

The little boy in the nursery was hidden in a huge cardboard box. He was brumming and screeching and the box moved from side to side.

'Ah,' said the school inspector, 'are you in your racing car?'

'No, I'm in a cardboard box,' replied the child.

Anon

My third son, Dominic, six at the time, was sitting with his family at the dinner table. He looked up with a thoughtful expression on his face.

'Mummy,' he said, 'what's a penis?'

His two older brothers nearly choked on their dinners.

'There's nothing to laugh at,' I told the boys. 'It's a perfectly reasonable question. And daddy will tell you what it is, Dominic, after you have finished dinner.' Later I endeavoured to explain this potentially tricky topic as clearly and fully as I could.

---

bellyful of words and do not know a thing. — Ralph Waldo Emerson

'Does that explain it?' I asked my son.

'No,' he replied. He looked thoroughly confused.

'Where did you hear the word "penis",' I asked.

'My teacher used it today in class.'

'I see, and she didn't explain what it was?'

'No, she just said a penis was coming into school to play the piano in the assembly tomorrow.'

Over the years I have visited schools, I have come to appreciate just how shrewd, bluntly honest and witty children can be. I was once approached by a small girl in the infant classroom who observed that 'when I am twenty-one, you'll probably be dead.

In an infant school in the Yorkshire Dales I was listening to a child read from the Beatrix Potter story of Peter Rabbit. He arrived at that part of the story when poor Peter Rabbit, trying to escape the terrifying Mr McGregor who was searching for him in the vegetable garden, had become entangled in the gooseberry net. The frightened little rabbit had given himself up for lost and was shedding big tears.

'What a terrible thing it would be,' I said, 'if poor Peter Rabbit should be caught.'

'Rabbits! Rabbits!' cried the angry-faced little lad, scratching his tangled mop of hair in irritation. 'They're a blasted nuisance, that's what my dad says! Have you seen what rabbits do to a rape crop?'

Public schools are the nurseries of all vice and

I answered that I had not. 'We shoot 'em!'
'We gas ours,' added the little girl who was sitting next to him.

The rabbit has a charming face,
Its private life is a disgrace,.
I really dare not name to you
The awful things that rabbits do.

Anon

I taught infants in a small rural primary school in Derbyshire. One memory concerns Charlie. If an angel were to descend to earth it would have the countenance of that little six-year-old. He had golden curls, skin as smooth as marble, great wide eyes and the most angelic expression. Coming into school one winter's day, his cheeks red with cold, he announced, 'It's snowing effing fireworks out there.'

Eleanor Radcliffe

'And what,' asked the teacher, 'was the message that Jesus gave to his disciples and followers after he had given 'The Sermon on the Mount' and fed the five thousand?'
'Remember to take your litter home with you,' replied a child.

Anon

---

immorality. — Henry Fielding (1707-1754)

And they were bringing children to him, that he might touch them; and the disciples rebuked them. But when Jesus saw it he was indignant, and said to them, 'Let the children come to me, do not hinder them; for to such belongs the kingdom of God. Truly, I say to you, whoever does not receive the kingdom of God like a child shall not enter it.'

Mark, Chapter 10, Verses 13–16

My wife's great grandfather, Joseph Bentley, author of *How to Sleep on a Windy Night* (a Bible commentary) and father of thirteen children, was a noted preacher in the Yorkshire Methodist circuit. He founded the Bradford Coffee Houses in an attempt to counter the ruinous effects of strong drink.

On one occasion, so we are told, he was preaching to the chapel congregation, which contained a number of children who sat on the front pew. He addressed himself to the children and was warning them of the deviousness of the Devil and how he could tempt them into doing wrong, when a fly landed on the lectern before him.

'And the Devil can lure you into sin,' he proclaimed, 'as sure as I swot this fly.'

He lifted up his hand and brought it down with a resounding smack. He missed and the fly buzzed off.

He smiled. 'Well happen there's hope for you yet,' he said.

'Manners are not taught in lessons,' said Alice.

'And Ruth in the Bible,' said the vicar, 'walked behind the
reapers picking up the corn which they had dropped. Can anyone
tell me what they call that?'

'Nicking,' replied a pupil.

The infant came in from the playground with mournful expression on his
small face. He was shivering with the cold and had a glistening frozen
teardrop on his cheek.

'Aaaaah,' sighed the teacher. 'Have you been crying?'

The child shook his head.

'You have, haven't you?' said the teacher with the most sympathetic of smiles.
'You've been crying. Here, let me wipe that little teardrop away.' She gently
brushed the child's cheek with a finger.

The child stared her straight in the eyes. 'It's snot,' he told her.

A schoolmaster, who was trying to discover what his class of
boys knew of common objects, asked what it was a horse was
made to wear when it went about its work. There was no reply
and the word 'harness' for which he sought was not forthcoming.

So he said: 'Is there any boy here whose father attends to
horses?'

'Yes, sir,' said one small boy.

'Then tell the class, George, what it is that your father puts on a

— *Lewis Carroll*, 'Through the Looking-Glass'

Better than a thousand days of diligent study is

horse every morning,' said the schoolmaster.

'A fiver each way,' was the reply.

F Norman

Teacher: 'If I lay two eggs here and one there, what will I have?'
Pupil: 'A miracle.'

The visitor noticed how well-mannered was the boy sitting opposite him in the dining room, how he chewed slowly with mouth closed, occasionally dabbed the corners of his lips and, when his meal was finished, how he placed his knife and fork together.

'You have very good table manners, young man,' the visitor told the boy. 'I noticed that, unlike some of the other children, you didn't put your elbows on the table.'

'If I did that at home,' replied the child, 'my father would say, "All joints will be carved".'

A child should always say what's true,
And speak when he is spoken to,
And behave mannerly at table
At least as far as he is able.

Robert Louis Stevenson, A Child's Garden of Verses *(1885)*

---

one day with a great teacher. — Japanese proverb

Teacher: 'Where is Hadrian's Wall?'
Pupil: 'Round Hadrian's garden.'

The children lined the street waving flags and cheering. They waited excitedly for the appearance of Princess Diana who was visiting the town. When she appeared she looked every inch the princess of the fairy tale: beautiful, elegant, smiling warmly and dressed in the most stunning outfit. As she walked down the line of children receiving the many bouquets, she caught sight of a small, grubby little boy holding a couple of wilting flowers. The princess was known for her kindness and knew how to relate to children. She approached the boy, took the flowers from him, ruffled his hair and asked if he had the day off school to come and see her.
'No,' he replied, 'I'm off with nits.'

The school nurse came to examine the children's heads for lice. One outspoken pupil, with carefully combed locks, objected, telling her he didn't like anyone touching his hair.
'Everyone has to have their head examined for nits,' explained the nurse.
'Not everyone,' replied the child.
'Yes, everyone.'
'Well what about Buddhists then?'

Education is what remains when we have forgotten all that we

Head teacher: 'And what do you know about the broken window, Carruthers?'

Pupil: 'Well, I didn't do it, Sir, but if it was me it was an accident.'

The visitor had been invited into school to talk to the children about his experiences during the war when he was evacuated. He was showing them his father's medals and the beret with the regimental badge on the front.

'And at home somewhere, I have the gas mask in a small square cardboard box. I used to wear it on a string around my neck. That was in case of a gas attack. I was looking for it this morning to bring in to show you but couldn't find it. I had an idea it was behind the tank in the attic.'

'You have a tank in your attic?' exclaimed a child.

In an effort to economise, a prudent headmaster, among other economies, instructed the caretaker to replace all the soft toilet tissues in the school lavatories with Izal, that shiny, sterile and malodorous paper popular in the past.

One small girl, rushing out of the toilets, exclaimed to her teacher: 'I can't possibly go to the toilet. There's only tracing paper in there!'

have been taught. — George Savile, Marquis of Halifax (1633-1695)

Letter from a child to the bishop who had visited the school and explained, among other things, the symbolism of his crozier:
'Dear Bishop, Thank you for coming into our school. I now know what a crook looks like.'

Thank-you letter from a child to the site manager after a school visit to a building site:
'Dear Mr Gibson, Thank you for letting us visit the building site. It was really interesting and I learnt a lot of words that I hadn't heard before.'

Gemma came home from school to tell her mother that the boys kept asking her to do handstands against the wall. Her mother told her not to do this because it was just so they could see her knickers.
'I know that,' replied the child, 'that's why I keep them in my schoolbag.'

'Why do you think it is important in a democratic society for people to have elections?' asked the teacher in a civics lesson.
'Because if men didn't have them,' replied the boy, 'they couldn't have kids.'

Education consists mainly in what we have unlearned. — Mark Twain

Chapter Five

THEN THERE ARE THE PARENTS

Children aren't happy with nothing to ignore,
That's what parents were created for.

Ogden Nash

The head teacher was confronted by a round, shapeless woman with bright frizzy blonde hair, an impressive set of double chins and immense hips. She had a ruddy complexion, heavy sleepy eyes and a mouth which turned downwards as if in perpetual hostility.

'Can I 'ave a word, Mrs Gardiner,' she said angrily.

'I am a little busy at the minute, Mrs Braithwaite,' replied the head teacher.

'Yes, well you might be, but this is himportant.'

'It always is, Mrs Braithwaite,' sighed Mrs Gardiner.

'Eh?'

'What seems to be the problem this time?'

Education is ... hanging around until you've caught on. — Robert Frost

Parents are precisely the people not to have children. — Anon

'Our Tequila came 'ome yesterday wi'out 'er Christmas bobbles. She had 'em in 'er 'air yesterday morning when she come to school and she come 'ome wi'out 'em. Somebody's gone an' nicked 'em off of 'er.'

'We can't be certain about that,' replied the head teacher. 'They might have fallen out when she was running around in the playground.'

'No, they didn't!' snapped Tequila's mother. 'I tied 'em on right tight. She come 'ome wi'out 'em, rooarin' 'er eyes out. They was new, them bobbles. Just bought 'em from t' market.'

'And what do these Christmas bobbles look like?' enquired Mrs Gardiner.

'Well, they was red Father Christmases wi' winking eyes. I didn't shell out good money to 'ave 'em nicked.'

'We will have a good look round for them, Mrs Braithwaite, and now if you will excuse me, I am rather busy.'

'No!' cried Tequila's mother. 'That won't do. It won't do at all. Somebody's nicked 'er bobbles and I want 'em findin'. It's 'appened before. My Tequila's come 'ome without other things which 'ave gone missing, like her Mickey Mouse knickers for one thing.'

'Mrs Braithwaite,' said the head teacher sharply. 'Leave the matter with me and I will make inquiries. Now I really must ask you …'

The woman was not to be put off. 'Well, I wants to know what you are going to do.'

'Well, let me see,' said Mrs Gardiner calmly. 'Tomorrow, I shall get the teachers, the classroom assistants, the dinner ladies, the mid-day

---

Angry parent to the teacher: 'You couldn't teach 'em if we didn't 'ave 'em!'

supervisors, the cleaners, the lollipop lady, the caretaker and all the children to search for Tequila's Christmas bobbles which must have cost you all of two pounds. We will stop all the lessons to look high and low and we will leave no stone unturned until we have found them.'

Mrs Braithwaite paused for a moment before replying, 'Are you taking the piss?'

> It is no use transferring our responsibility and guilt to the youngsters themselves. It is we who have made them what they are, and who have failed to prevent them becoming what they are.
>
> *Sir Alec Clegg*

A FATHER'S ADVICE TO HIS SON

Always smile at those you meet
And they will do the same.
Look for good in others, son,
And don't waste time on blame.
Never be ashamed of crying,
It's not a sign you're weak,
And don't be quick to criticise
And think before you speak.
Give more than you take, my son,
Do no one hurt or harm

And don't be afraid of being wrong
And always chance your arm.
Stick firmly to your principles,
Don't follow fads and trends,
And always answer to your heart
And value all your friends.
And keep that sense of humour
It will help you to survive
And don't take life too seriously, son,
For none come out alive.

Schoolteachers are not fully appreciated by parents

A lecturer, giving a talk on the dangers of overpopulation, asked his audience if they realised that every minute of every day a woman was giving birth to a child somewhere in the world.

'And what are we going to do about it?' he asked.

'Find the woman and tell her to stop,' came a voice from the audience.

I've never got over the parents' evening when I took one of my twins and had a nice chat with the teacher about her progress, and then asked after her twin sister. There was an embarrassed silence followed by the teacher asking, 'What, are there two of them?'

I recall going to my youngest daughter's parents' evening and her teacher giving me teachers' speak about her performance and I said, 'so is she about average ability?' to which the teacher replied, 'Oh we don't measure them like that. What we do is blah, blah, blah...' and I said, 'I wouldn't have minded if you said she wasn't,' to which the teacher gave an embarrassed smile.

I attended my son's first year parents' evening at his comprehensive and the French teacher gave a scathing account of him — and then to my amazement awarded him the Year Seven form prize for his performance.

until it rains all day Saturday. — E C McKenzie

'If you don't believe all the things your daughter tells you that happen at school,' said the teacher, to the parent, 'then I won't believe all the things your daughter tells me that happen at home.'

At the parents' evening Richard's teacher passed his exercise book across the table. She pointed to a part of the account he had written entitled: 'What we did over the weekend.'
'On Saturday night my daddy beat my mummy again.'
The teacher raised an eyebrow.
'Scrabble,' I said. 'I beat my wife at Scrabble.'

I spent most of my career working in a social priority South Yorkshire pit village. One parents' evening I was singing the praises of the parents' son, an ex-pupil of mine.
'I hope you get my other lad next year,' she said. 'He's a little git.'
Choosing to overlook the indiscretion, I informed her that I was retiring.
'F***** hell,' came the reply.

Diane French

At the parents' evening I wanted to give the impression that I, as a new teacher (wet behind the ears), knew what I was about. I had a boy in my class, a quiet, biddable young man who was

I'm not terribly worried about young people. It's the

experiencing some problems with his work. His father and mother listened attentively as I explained how I intended to help him.

'He may of course have a touch of dyslexia,' I told them, 'or maybe dyspraxia' (terms I had come across at college but knew precious little about). I then proceeded to tell them, at some length, how they might help him at home. The parents said little, thanked me and departed. I was later to discover that the couple both worked in education: the mother was a lecturer at the university, the father a head teacher.

Daniel McNeil

The headmaster would show prospective parents around the school. If there was a room he didn't wish the visitors to see he would put a sign on the door: 'Quiet Please! Oxbridge Examination in Progress.' He would handpick students to assist, drilling them into saying that they enjoyed school, were doing well in their studies and telling them not to forget to comment on the good teaching and excellent resources.

C P

I was head teacher of a small preparatory school. I believed that all the children in my care mattered, that their lives should be enriched, that success on which a teacher could build must

parents who frighten me the most. — Lord Shawcross

be found for every child and that encouragement is more
important than punishment. For me the keys to success in a child's
life are self-esteem and expectation. Over the years I have met
many hardworking, dedicated and supportive parents who want
the very best for their children but there are a few who are ignorant
and unfeeling.

I shall never forget an interview I had with a parent who wished
to send his daughter to the school. The father was a loud, bullish
individual. He sat in my office with his daughter — a small, pale,
little girl of eight, and proceeded to tell me what he expected
of me and the teachers, telling me that his son, away at school,
was a gifted student destined for great things. He then, looking
at his daughter, told me that she was shy and not 'blessed with
much up top' and would need special help. Having listened to
him for quite long enough I asked if I might speak to his daughter.

'Now,' I said to the child, 'could you tell me something about
yourself and what you are good at?'

The girl looked up at her father and said the saddest thing
I have heard in my entire teaching career.

'Well I'm not much good at anything really,' she said. 'Father
says I'm a bit of a disappointment.'

Christine Mason

You will find as the children grow up that as a rule children are a bitter disappointment — their greatest object being to do precisely what their parents do not wish and have anxiously tried to prevent.

Queen Victoria, 'Letters and Journals', 5th January, 1876

A family was called in to see the head teacher about their son's foul language. They were very shame-faced and apologetic. 'I don't know where he gets it from,' said his mother. 'It must be them buggers next door.'

Diane French

The visitor noticed an old, clumsily made tray on the Georgian sideboard; it looked completely out of place amid the expensive antique furniture in the beautifully furnished house.

'I see you looking at the tray,' said his host. 'It is the most costly item in the room.'

'Really?' said the visitor.

'You see I sent my son to one of the most prestigious public schools in the country. It cost me £30,000 a year in fees. He was there for four years so I shelled out in total £120,000. When he left the only exam he passed was woodwork — hence the tray.'

the father, 'provided, that is, you are up when they get in.'

The most misspelled word I received in letters from parents was 'diarrhoea':
   'Please excuse Deborah from PE as she had diahoeah which is all down our street.'
   'John has been off with dire rear.'

   'Jason was off school because he has diah … diarrh … dhiarr — the shits.'

   A very stout mother arrived at the head teacher's office on the second floor of a large city school one day, so out of breath from the exertion of climbing the stairs that for a short time she was completely speechless.
   The headmistress waited until she had recovered her breath, and then asked what she could do for her.
   'Ah've come to say our Mary won't be at school today, 'cos she's got diarrhoea.'
   The headmistress thanked her for calling, but tactfully pointed out that she could have sent a note instead. The mother's reply was brief but forthright:
   'Do you think I'd have climbed all your bloomin' stairs if I could have spelt that word?'

Education: a process which makes one rogue cleverer than another. — Oscar Wilde

A parent sent back to school two books, given by the teacher, which she felt unsuitable for her nine-year-old to read. They were called *Naughty Boys and Naughty Girls* and *Before we go to Bed*. Both books were by Enid Blyton.

Letters to teachers from parents have sometimes brought a smile to the recipients' lips:

'Wayne has a new motorbike. Please may he park it at the back of the classroom?'

'Janice has come home with nits and they're not hers.'

'Deborah was absent yesterday because I kept her off school. She spent the evening with the scouts and is very tired.'

'Jason was off of school last week because he had a germ in his plonker.'

'Dear Mrs Pearson,
You have my permission to hit Donald if he is naughty. When I was at school there was the cane, and I had it most weeks. In my opinion they ought to bring back capital punishment.'

To teach is to learn twice over. — Joseph Joubert

'Dear Mrs Talbot,

Would you please not write to me again about Simon's absence on the 31st June? After such a long time I cannot remember — so take your pick:

> Cough
> Cold
> Gone fishing with Dad
> Gone shopping with me
> Broken his leg
> At a funeral
> Thought it was a Saturday
> House on fire
> Tsunami.'

'I'm sorry Shirley wasn't at school yesterday, but while I was out she had the baby.'

'Jennifer will not attend school for the next two weeks as we are going on holiday. I hope this does not interfere with your plans for industrial action.'

'Please excuse Dean from games. He's a pain in the downstairs department.'

Education: one of the chief obstacles to intelligence

'Debbie tells me she is being asked to help other children with their reading. I don't like her being treated as another pair of hands to listen to other children read.'

'Unfortunately, Jason's coursework has been destroyed by the girl whose hamster he put in the washing machine.'

'My son should not be kept back after class to do his French homework. I do not approve of the French language. English is the language he should know, not French.'

'I can't see the point of Melanie learning Shakespeare. She needs to learn proper English.'

'Mrs Atkinson, as I said, I can't read english [sic] books to Rebecca so please don't sent [sic] them home. She only gets upset. After all, its [sic] your job to teach her to read and not mine.'
'I got your letter about my Stanley needing to come to school clean and about him smelling. It's your job to teach him, not to smell him.'

A letter from the head teacher to parents, Brampton New National School (1871):
You must remember that you have not done all that is required

---

and freedom of thought. — Bertrand A Russell

by merely gaining admission for your child into our school. Do not suppose that its education is to be left entirely to the care of the master or mistress, and that you are to do nothing. Unless you labour together with them for your child's welfare, disappointment to all parties will be the result.

Much of the impertinence, bad language and ill-behaviour which so disgrace and degrade the youth of our town, and of which continual complaint is made, is, in too many cases, to be traced to the want of due care in setting a good example and enforcing it at home; and not as is falsely and wickedly attributed to the fault of the school.

From Mr A Storey, head teacher to parents, Hayfield School, Doncaster (2005):
We were somewhat bemused last week to be asked (9.15am phone call) by a parent to 'send a car' to collect her child as the family had 'overslept' and hence missed the school bus and by her apparent angst that we had no one available to provide this service! Sadly, we don't have a member of staff or vehicle idling on tap to pick up the outcomes of slumber excess; go to collect John's packed lunch or PE shorts; deliver a house key to Auntie Mabel; take Anne to the dentist. Nor is our Attendance Monitoring secretary on call to undertake a morning pick up service. Sorry about that!

Give a man a fish and you feed him for a day; teach a man

PARENTS' EVENING

So you are Matthew's mother,
Then you must be his dad?
I'm very pleased to meet you,
I am extremely glad.

He's such a gifted pupil,
And such a little dear,
There's been a vast improvement
In all his work this year.

His writing is exceptional,
So beautifully neat,
His spelling quite incredible,
His poetry a treat.

His number work is flawless
And his painting so inspired.
He's interested and lively,
And he's never ever tired.

He's amazingly athletic,
He excels in every sport.

Your Matty is the brightest child
That I have ever taught.

I should say he's gifted,
He comes top in every test.
In fact, in every single subject
Your Matthew is the best!

I must say Mr and Mrs Flynn,
You're fortunate to have a child like him.
Pardon?

Oh, you're not Matthew Flynn's father,
Then you can't be his mum.
You say I've got the names mixed up.
Oh dear! What have I done?

Well, I'm very very sorry.
So your child's Matthew Brown.
Well, before I tell you about your son,
You had better both sit down!

---

to fish and you feed him for a lifetime. — Maimonides

Chapter Six

MUST TRY HARDER

My mother was a bit of a hoarder. When she died I discovered all my old school reports in a blue folder. They made interesting and sometimes surprising reading. They show that I was 'fairly good' or 'good' in most things and rather better in English. Reading through them now I get the impression that my teachers saw me as a decent enough boy but one of average intelligence and limited prospects.

I am described in tones that strike me as deeply condescending, a way of saying I would not achieve much in life. As can been seen from my final junior school report, my form teacher's comments and the head teacher's observations are far from extensive. Teachers these days, obliged to write detailed assessments of a child's achievement, effort, progress and conduct which cover a good few pages, must view such an unforthcoming end of school report with wry humour.

Intelligence plus character — that is the goal

Broom Valley Primary School Rotherham
School Report for Gervase Phinn
July, 25th, 1958.   Class 4.   Number in class: 43.

Subject	Max. marks	Marks obtained	Comment
ENGLISH			
Reading	20	20	Very Good
Composition	20	18	Good
Spelling	20	12	Needs care
Language & Literature	20	15	Fair
Comprehension	20	17	Quite Good
ARITHMETIC			
Mental	20	11	Must try harder
Accuracy	50	44	Good
Problems	30	25	Good
HISTORY	20	14	Very interested. Disappointing result.
GEOGRAPHY	20	17	Very Good
NATURE STUDY SCIENCE	20	18	Very Good
CRAFTWORK			Fair
MUSIC			Fair
ART			Fairly Good
PT & GAMES			Fairly Good
CONDUCT			Very Good
PROGRESS			Gervase is a steady worker, always trying his best. He shows an interest in all activities.

Head teacher: *J Leslie Morgan*

---

of true education. — Martin Luther King Jr

This is a revealing report, not because it tells you very much about the pupil's attainment and progress, but because it indicates, in its paucity and restraint, the sort of information parents were likely to receive about their child's education in the 1950s. It was perhaps thought by the teachers that it was not good for pupils to be too cocksure, so there was no fulsome praise or hearty congratulations. However, I should have thought that the full marks I achieved for Reading might have merited an 'excellent' and the 18 out of 20 for composition a 'very good.'

The very mention of the school report takes us back to our childhood and to the first time outside our family when we were judged, hopefully in praiseworthy terms but sometimes unfairly, often critically.

One experience I shared with some friends was that we tend to look back with somewhat rose-tinted spectacles when we recall our time at school and the glowing reports we received. It therefore comes as something of a shock when we discover that we were not that good after all. Having looked at my son's GCSE English essay one evening, I commented to Dominic that his spelling needed attention, adding pompously that the one thing I was always very good at when I was his age was spelling. He discovered my school report in the loft some weeks later and showed me, with a wry smile, what Mr Dyeball had written on my school report prior to my taking the GCE: 'Gervase writes with originality but his spelling is in need of attention.'

Education makes people easy to lead but difficult to drive;

Edward Collier writing in the Guardian *had a similar sobering experience:*

The remarks of my old teachers were a revelation. I had no idea how poorly I had performed academically. It turns out I was dismally underachieving, bobbing around in the bottom quarter. I've lived all my adult life believing I could be a contender, and it's a bit of a shock that I wasn't even a journeyman.

He lists some of the comments his former teachers made about him:

Untidy, casual and insufficient (age 9)

Has not learned to concentrate his attention on anything yet (age 9)

Work is too brief, casual and untidily executed (age 11)

Edward tries sometimes, but most of the time is satisfied with as little work as possible (age 11)

Has no idea how to be helpful, and the thought of work appals him (age 11).

School reports of the past tended to be short, blunt and more interesting to read. They could also be sarcastic, hurtful and derisory. Teachers often vied with each other to compose something they felt was clever and witty — a smart turn of phrase. The *Telegraph* published the fifteen most cutting school reports sent in by the readers. These included the staggeringly offensive:

'He has emitted slight signs of life recently.'

'This boy has delusions of adequacy.'

---

easy to govern, but impossible to enslave. — Lord Brougham

'Words fail me. No work, no effort, no apparent concern.'
'If ignorance is bliss, this boy's happiness must be colossal.'
'Displays his ignorance with enthusiasm.'
'He has contributed much during his time here, some of it helpful.'
'Intellectually indolent.'

I was amazed to find, when asking friends and relatives about their school reports, that it was a common practice for teachers of the past to make such caustic comments:

'Thomas is likely to go down in history — and English and geography.'

'Martin has an answer for everything. Unfortunately for him he fails to understand the questions.'

'If Linda spent more time on her work and less time chattering, preening herself and interfering with others, she might actually achieve something.'

'Attainment poor, effort poor, concentration poor, behaviour poor. There is nothing else to say.'

'Barely satisfactory in English and history. Unsatisfactory in everything else.'

'A lazy boy of lacklustre academic ability.'

'The class comedian who will not find it very funny when he fails all his exams.'

Do not train a child to learn by force or harshness; but direct

'Patrick sets low personal standards and then consistently fails to achieve them.'

I had a vindictive dislike of grown-up persons who tried to be witty at my expense.
Arthur Ransome

I had the pleasure of speaking at a literary lunch in York alongside the best-selling and award-winning novelist and playwright Beryl Bainbridge who confided in me that her school report in English (like mine) noted her problem with spelling: 'Though her written work is the product of an obviously lively imagination, it is a pity that her spelling derives from the same source.'

The pleasure of reading the reports of the great and good and those others who have gone on to be successful in life is realising that their teachers very often were deemed to be poor at predicting how their young charges would get on in the wide world. As Oliver Wendell Holmes remarked: 'The world's great men have not commonly been scholars, nor great scholars great men.'

I was sent away to school and my parents, who were abroad for most of the time, were never able to make it to parents' evenings and open days so they lived in blissful ignorance of what I was like at school. I would tell them how I was getting on famously, working

them to it by what amuses their minds. — Plato

hard and doing well in my studies. During the school holidays the school report would arrive. I knew it was coming so I waited for the postman at the gate. I recognised the letter by the school's fancy crest on the envelope. I would take the report, invariably bad, and ceremoniously burn it in the bathroom, flushing the remains down the toilet bowl. Some of the comments by my teachers were downright cruel and sarcastic, along the lines of 'One wonders if John is in this world or the next'; or 'he spends most of the lessons in a state of joyful lethargy.' The headmaster's terse comment at the end of one report was particularly galling: 'John must bestir himself.' Years later when I qualified in medicine I had the pleasure of seeing my former headmaster as a patient. I was tempted to tell him I had indeed bestirred myself to good effect.

Dr Jeremy T Wilson

I was amused by this letter in my local paper:
    'To Mr Smith who said at school I was a waste of space and that I would not come to anything in life. If you are in the South of France do come and visit me at my villa in Vence. Then we can take a trip on my yacht and talk over old times.'

John Metcalfe

The great aim of education is not knowledge but action. — Herbert Spencer

One particularly nasty teacher wrote on my report that I was 'a rather sly boy'. I might have been many things when I was at school but I was never sly. The comment hurt. I had been accused, the week before the report was written, of copying parts of my essay from a book. The teacher, Mr Talbot, felt it was too good to be my own work. I took the report home, steamed open the envelope and altered 'a rather sly boy' to 'a rather shy boy'. I guess with hindsight that it was rather devious of me to alter the comment, but at the time I felt fully justified. When my father read that I was 'a rather shy boy' he shook his head and sighed, 'Well, you certainly have quite enough to say for yourself at home.'

Rev Michael Brown

Here are some school reports of the famous who proved very successful, despite their former teachers' comments:

Clement Attlee — 'His chief fault is that he is very self-opinionated, so much so that he gives very scant consideration to the views of other people.'

Arthur Marshall — 'Does well to find his way home.'

Sir Peter Ustinov — 'He shows great originality, which must be curbed at all costs.'

Joanna Lumley — 'She must learn to speak politely when her requests are refused.'

Children and drunks speak the truth.

Cilla Black — 'Priscilla is suitable for office work.'

Diana, Princess of Wales — 'She must try to be less emotional in her dealings with others.'

Dame Judi Dench — 'Judi would be a very good pupil if she lived in this world.'

John Lennon — 'Certainly on the road to failure.'

Siegfried Sassoon — 'Lacks power of concentration. Shows no particular intelligence or aptitude for any branch of his work.'

Sir Winston Churchill's report from St George's School is uninspiring to say the least:

'Is a constant trouble to everybody and is always in some scrape or other.'

'He cannot be trusted to behave himself anywhere.'

'He has no ambition.'

'Composition very feeble.'

'Spelling about as bad as it well can be.'

Robert Graves's last memory of school was the headmaster's parting shot:

'Well, goodbye, Graves, and remember that your best friend is the waste paper basket.'

(Graves went on to become one of the country's most celebrated writers.)

I believe it is better to restrain children by the feeling

of shame and by kindness than by fear. — Terence

Sometimes, a teacher, struggling to find anything good to say about a child, writes such a feeble comment that it can be as hurtful as the harsher kind:
'Quite a useful member of the class.'
'A biddable girl, as far as I know.'
'Peggy has been a big help as the milk monitor this term.'
'Although Barry is clearly no scholar he tries his best.'
'A cheerful little plodder.'

Some school reports do bring a smile to the lips:
'Clive's science is spoilt by dirty drawings.'
'She can read well and already knows a number of four-letter words.' (Infant report.)
'Robert is immature.' (Infant report.)
'John's reading test score would have improved if he had read more accurately.'

It was the practice at one boarding school for all the new boys to be given a medical examination on entry and at the end of the first year. They were weighed and their heights measured. It was discovered at the end-of-year medical that one pupil had not grown at all but in fact he had shrunk by an inch. The housemaster, thinking of something positive to write about the boy, decided upon: 'William has settled down well this year.'

At home a boy can learn only those things which are taught him; in school he

Today, teachers have to be very careful in what they say about a pupil so their reports tend to be sober, restrained and bland and are often full of educational jargon. Some are just lifted from a bank of computerised statements and could be about any child. There is little personal comment. Teachers these days are rarely rude or sarcastic about their pupils for they know that they might be confronted with an aggrieved parent on the consultation evening.

The reports now tend to gloss over the pupils' failings, the teachers worried that any adverse comment about a child will risk upsetting the parent. I cannot count the numbers of occasions on a parents' evening, coming face-to-face with a disgruntled mother or father of a particularly difficult and disruptive child on whose report I had written 'he needs to be better behaved in class', to be told angrily, 'Well he's not like that at home.'

One of the most supportive of reports on a student was that written on Michelangelo. Going to Rome to see the Pope prior to his being employed to build the great dome of St Peter's and paint the Sistine Chapel, the young painter took with him the report given to him by his teacher which said:

'The bearer of these presents is Michelangelo, the sculptor … His nature is such that he requires to be drawn out by kindness and encouragement — but if love be shown him and he be treated really well, he will accomplish things that will make the whole world wonder.'

Now wouldn't we all like a report like that?

---

learns also from what is taught to others. — Marcus Fabious Quintilian

Chapter Seven

THE SCHOOL INSPECTOR CALLS

SCHOOL INSPECTOR
Inspector —
Cold eyes,
Sharp white teeth,
Smiles like a crocodile,
Frightens the teacher
Who stands
Trembling.

The notice of an OFSTED (Office for Standards in Education) inspection makes most teachers at the very least apprehensive and at worst terrified. A team of school inspectors descend on a school and examine every aspect of the education therein: leadership and management, efficiency, governance, resources, premises, punctuality, absences, the provision of spiritual, moral, social and cultural development, the quality of teachings, extra-curricular

---

The function of education is to teach one to think

activities, health and safety, sex education and a host of other things. They will see how well the school relates to parents, deals with bullying, promotes British values, how healthy the food is on offer and much more. In addition, each subject will be examined, the teachers observed and assessed. The report is then published and is in the public domain for all to read. No wonder teachers feel threatened. How times have changed.

In *HMI: Some passages in the life of one of HM Inspectors of Schools*, published in 1913, the wonderfully-named E M Sneyd-Kynnersley, formerly HMI in the North West Division, gives an interesting insight into the work of the school inspector at the turn of the twentieth century:

> What does the inspector have to do? There was the Elementary Education Act, 1870, to study and there were Instructions of the vaguest kind.
>
> In 1871 school inspection was, as a science, still in its infancy. The chief function of HM Inspector was to assess the right amount which the Treasury should pay; and this was done by rapid examination of every child above seven years of age who had attended 250 times in the school year.

Mr Sneyd-Kynnersely waxes somewhat lyrical about his function:

> 'Let it not be supposed that the modern style of inspector is wholly free from folly and vice. HMI are not generally beloved.

intensively and to think critically. — Martin Luther King Jr

It is a pleasant profession for a peaceably minded man. If I were asked to state its principal charm I should say it is irresponsibility. The income is moderate but sufficient and certain. In the dim and distant future looms the pension assuring bread and butter. The standard of comfort is therefore assured. Unfruitfulness of honest work does not threaten poverty. But the chief comfort is, there is no personal worry.'

His idiosyncratic and sometimes savage reports make interesting reading:

'Mrs Evans is getting rather middle-aged for the little ones; always motherly, but not always fresh and gamesome.'

'The condition of the school is far from satisfactory. The singing, which is the main object of interest, is even worse than at last year's inspection. Of the teachers, several should be contemplating acceptance of a retiring pension. The boys are ill-behaved and their musical capacity is on a level with their behaviour.'

'The children have two lessons a week, each of fifteen minutes on threading a needle. On Friday afternoon they had a lesson of riddles! Why does a miller wear a white hat? When is a door not a door? For children who have gone through a year of this course of instruction, including the cow, the camel and the cat, life has not further terrors and death comes as a happy relief.'

Children sweeten labours, but they make

misfortunes more bitter. — Francis Bacon

In the early days, at the conclusion of the inspection, the HMI would give
the teacher he had observed a certificate of competence. Mr Sneyd-Kynnersley, despite his sometimes highly critical reports, concludes that, 'A little
experience taught me that infants should be left in the hands of their teachers, and that the inspectors should look on.' The teachers of the early years
today would certainly not argue with that.

Mr Sneyd-Kynnersley continues:

> 'It was not thought fair to speak ill of a teacher on his
> certificate, unless there were special grounds. Therefore, one
> proceeded with judicious omission. If one read that Mr A 'taught
> the elementary subjects with fair success' one drew two inferences:
> (1) that he could not teach anything else; (2) that his discipline was
> weak, because it was not mentioned. But if it stated that Mrs B
> "maintained good order, and was particularly successful in
> teaching handwriting" it became obvious that her arithmetic was
> a deplorable failure.'

Early reports from the school inspectors indicated that many schools were
clearly failing the children — as this inspector reported after a visit to one
school in 1854:

> 'The affairs are ill-managed by a committee of languid,
> educationally inept amateurs and the school is staffed by

incompetent and unscrupulous teachers. To form the minds of children and direct their powers of reading into beneficial channels the teacher must know much more than is expressed in the lessons themselves.'

As is the case today, HMI reports would provide the information for Government reports on the state of education. In 1921 The Newbold Committee was set up to investigate the teaching of English in schools and painted a grim picture indeed. G Sampson, a member of the committee, gave in his evidence a description of a visit to an elementary school which was not uncommon:

'The children can make noises but they cannot speak … Go into a classroom and ask each boy and girl his name or her name and address. You will hardly understand the familiar names. You will understand none of the unfamiliar names … Ask a boy to tell you something about a game or a book or a place and he will struggle convulsively among words like a fly in a jam dish.'

I have to say that in my experience inspecting schools I have never come across a young child in a mainstream school who 'struggles with words like a fly in a jam dish'. Indeed, I have found the very opposite; young children were only too willing to ask questions and give their opinions. On one occasion I came across an infant who was diligently filling a plastic bucket with

an ill man worse. — seventeenth-century proverb

dry sand. I watched as she upended the bucket. The contents spilled out.

'What you need to do,' I told her, 'is to add some water to the sand and that will hold it together.'

'Don't want to,' replied the child sulkily.

'Adding a little water makes the sand stick, you see,' I told her.

'Don't want to,' repeated the child.

'Let me show you,' I said.

I took the bucket from the child and scooped up a handful of dry sand and filled it to the top. Then, ladling up some liquid in a small cup from a large tray containing water, I poured it into the bucket, mixed the contents and patted it down. The small girl watched me, screwing up her nose as if there was an unpleasant smell in the room. Upending the bucket and tapping the bottom I produced a perfect sandcastle. 'You see,' I said smiling. 'I used to make sandcastles like this one when I took my children to the beach. Now, you have a go.'

'Don't want to!' said the child emphatically and raising her voice. 'How many more times do I have to tell you?'

'Is there a reason why you don't want to, Rosie?' I asked.

'Because Jamie's wee'ed in the water tray, that's why!'

In a class of seven-year-olds an HMI approached a grubby but bright-eyed little boy splashing paint on to a large piece of sugar paper.

'Hullo, what are you doing?' he asked.

'How many teachers work here?' asked the inspector.

'Paintin'!' came the blunt reply.

'It looks very good.'

'We dunt paint much,' the child said. 'Only we are today. We've got an important visitor coming.' There was no thought in the boy's mind that the important visitor might be the school inspector.

'And what are you painting?' the HMI asked.

'It's a jungle,' came the reply. 'Prehistoric.'

'What's that creature?'

'Brontosaurus.'

'And that?'

'Triceratops. They 'ad three 'orns on their 'eads, tha' knows. Did tha' know that?'

'Yes.'

'This one's a pterodactyl and over 'ere's a pteranodon. A lot of people don't know t' difference, tha' knows. Do you?'

'Yes.'

'Well, a lot of people don't.'

'What's this one?' the inspector asked pointing to a round, fat, smiling creature.

'Stegosaurus. They had three brains, tha' knows.'

'Really?'

'One in their 'ead, one in their tail and one in their bum. It din't do 'em any good though.' The boy pointed to a vicious-looking monster with spikes

---

'About half of 'em,' replied the boy.

along its back and great sharp teeth like tank traps. 'He ate 'em all —
tyrannosaurus rex. He were reyt nasty, 'e was.'

'You know a lot about these creatures,' said the HMI.

'I know.' The little boy put down his brush. 'I luv 'em. They're great. I
draw 'em all t' time.'

'And are there any around today?'

'Course not! They're all dead. They're hextinct.'

'What does that mean?'

'Dead. Wiped aaht.'

'And why do you think that is?' the inspector asked.

The little boy thought for a moment. 'Well, mister,' he said, 'that's one of
life's gret mysteries, in't it?'

'This display looks very impressive,' said the school inspector, 'so colourful
and bright, with all the children's work so well-presented.'

'Yes,' replied the teacher, preening like a peacock, 'I must say I am very
pleased.'

'And he's been in all weekend putting it up specially,' said a pupil.

'Just for the inspector,' added another, 'because we don't normally have
a display on the wall, do we Sir?'

At one school I sat at the back of the classroom when an infant approached
me. 'Can you do add-ups?'

'Can you name this insect?' asked the school inspector.

'Yes,' I replied. 'I'm very good at add-ups.'

'And take-aways?'

'Good at those as well.'

'And timeses?'

'Excellent at timeses.'

'And guz-inters?'

'Guz-inters?' I repeated.

'You know, two guz-inter four, four guz-inter eight.'

'Ah, guz-inters!' I laughed. 'I'm outstanding at guz-inters.'

'Well, you shouldn't be sitting here,' said the girl. 'You should be on the top table.'

> 'Can you do Addition?' the White Queen asked. 'What's one and one and one and one and one and one and one and one and one and one?'
>
> 'I don't know,' said Alice. 'I lost count.'
>
> *Lewis Carroll*, Through the Looking-Glass

The former school inspector, Leonard Clarke, described a visit to a Yorkshire school in the 1950s. The head teacher asked him if he wanted to hear the children sing and the inspector soon found himself in the school hall where the senior choir were assembled to perform for him.

He enquired of the music teacher what the children were going to sing.

'Jason,' replied the child.

'Wetherby Socks,' replied the teacher, a large, bluff Yorkshireman.

'I don't know that particular tune,' said the inspector. 'Is it a local folk song?'

'Nay,' replied the teacher looking at him as if he were not quite right in the head, 'it's very famous. 'Asn't thy 'eard of it?'

'I can't say I have,' replied the inspector.

The music teacher turned to the choir which then gave an enthusiastic rendering of 'Where the Bee Sucks.'

You were expecting me, Mr Poppleton?

I think so … Miss … er …

Crindle.

I beg your pardon?

The name is Crindle. Miss Crindle.

Oh yes, Miss Crindle. I thought it was next Wednesday.

Next Wednesday?

That you were coming into school.

No, it was today. I wrote saying that I would be coming in today. Did you not get my letter, Mr Poppleton?

I'm sure I did Miss Crindle … somewhere … but I just can't lay my hands on it at the moment.

It was a very important letter, Mr Poppleton. It was an official letter in a brown envelope.

Yes, well I get a lot of letters, Miss Crindle. You see I'm a teaching head.

This is only a small school here in the Dales and I have to deal with letters and such when I can.

I appreciate that, Mr Poppleton, but ...

Well, now that you're here, Miss Crindle, where would you like to start? With the infants and work up, or with the juniors and work down?

I should like to start with you, Mr Poppleton.

With me?

I wish to discuss with you the composition of the catchment area, the new National Curriculum guidelines, the assessment, recording and reporting of pupil achievement, your school development plan, the anti-bullying policy, the provision you make for children from the ethnic minorities, the education of the traveller children, aspects of the rural schools project, early years mathematics teaching, school efficiency and management, the test results and your targets for the coming year. Then I should like ...

Waaaaaa! Hang on! Hang on, Miss Crindle. I don't have all that information at my fingertips you know.

Well don't you think you ought to, Mr Poppleton? After all, you are the head teacher.

Have you any idea what I do, Miss Crindle? I've got document after document coming over the Yorkshire Dales like the plagues of Egypt. I've got a faulty boiler, leaking roof, rising damp and toilets that don't flush. I've children with scabies, governors I never see and parents on my back all the time. I've got a teacher off with severe stress and another who has just

---

always like being taught. — Winston Churchill

returned from a training course and is about ready to chuck herself down a pothole at Gaping Gill. I've got …

Nevertheless, Mr Poppleton, I am obliged to speak to you on all these matters.

Well it's a new one on me, Miss Crindle. It's the first time in all my thirty-five years of teaching that the nit nurse has asked for that kind of information.

I am not the nit nurse. I am one of Her Majesty's Inspectors of Schools. Where are you going, Mr Poppleton?

To chuck myself down a pothole at Gaping Gill, Miss Crindle.

'How many sheep can you see in that field?' asked the school inspector intent on testing the Dales child on his number work.

'All of 'em,' replied the boy.

The children in a Yorkshire primary school were studying the Tudors. 'Can you tell me the names of any of Henry VIII's wives?' asked the school inspector.

'Aye, I can,' replied the child. 'There was Katherine of Arrogate and Ann of Leeds.'

The boy stood outside the classroom. The school inspector asked him why he had been sent out.

'Gross insolence, Sir,' replied the boy.

The young man was well-dressed and appeared very polite.

'What did you say?' asked the inspector.

'It wasn't what I said, Sir,' the boy told him. 'It was what I wrote.'

'And what did you write?'

'We were asked to write an essay: "Imagine you are a new-born baby and describe your first week in the world". I wrote three sides of "Glug, glug, glug".'

'And what is this word?' the school inspector asked.

'Can't you read?' asked the girl.

'I am not sure about this word: EGOG.'

"Edgehog,' explained the child.

I well recall the first school governing body I addressed as an OFSTED inspector. The serious-faced group sat before me, all eyes trained in my direction. The chair of governors, a florid-faced man with huge ginger eyebrows which curved into question marks, eyed me suspiciously with pale watery eyes.

'We're 'ere for the report from the school inspector,' he announced. 'This is Mr Flynn from OFFSET.'

---

are more deadly in the long run. — Mark Twain

'Off what?' enquired a plain-faced little woman with a pursed mouth and small black darting eyes.

'No, no, that's the water, Doris. Mr Flynn's from OFFSET.'

'OFSTED,' I corrected him, 'and it's Mr Phinn.'

'OFSTED?' he repeated, 'is that what it is?'

'OFFSET is, as I remember, a machine which prints paper,' I told him.

'Yes,' said the chair of governors, addressing me with a smile on his face, 'and looking at t' pile o' papers in front of us, I think OFFSET is about right.'

I wonder if Mr Sneyd-Kynnersely had as much enjoyment as I when he inspected schools. I very much doubt it.

I was coaching the hockey team when one of the girls said there was a strange man in a raincoat watching from the side-lines. She said she had seen him hanging about the school gate that morning and looking suspicious. I went over to the man.

'What exactly are you doing?' I asked him sharply.

'I'm watching the girls playing hockey,' he replied.

'I've heard of men like you,' I told him. 'Now on your way or I'll call the police.'

'I should have introduced myself,' he said, 'but I didn't want to interrupt the game. I'm one of the school inspectors.'

Janice Moore

Education is an admirable thing, but it is well to remember from time

THE SCHOOL INSPECTOR CALLS

Miss, Miss, there's a man at the back of the classroom,
With a big black book and a smile like a crocodile.
Miss, he asked me if I've got any homework,
And when I said, 'Too much!' — he wrote it down.

Miss, Miss, there's a man at the back of the classroom,
With a long, sharp pencil and eyes like a basking shark.
Miss, he asked me what I liked best about school
And when I said 'the dinners!' — he wrote it down.

Miss, Miss, there's a man at the back of the classroom,
With a big square badge and hair like a hedgehog.
Miss, I asked him what he liked best about our school
And he said he was not there to answer my questions,
He said he was just 'a fly on the wall'.

Miss, Miss, why don't you tell him to 'BUZZ OFF?'

---

to time that nothing worth knowing can be taught. — Oscar Wilde

Chapter Eight

ARE WE NEARLY THERE YET?

SCHOOL TRIP

On our school trip to Scarborough
We got to school on time,
But the coach was caught in traffic
And arrived at half past nine.
Miss Phipps, our teacher, was so cross,
Left standing in the rain
And when the coach pulled up at last
She didn't half complain.
The driver started shouting,
He said there'd been a queue,
But Miss Phipps she said, 'That's no
     excuse!'
And started shouting too.

On our school trip to Scarborough
The sky turned cold and grey,
Freezing winds blew down the beach
And it rained and rained all day.
Then Sharon slipped on a slimy rock,
And Gordon grazed his knee,
And Colin fell off the castle wall,
And John jumped in the sea.
Then our teacher started shouting
And her voice was loud and high,
And soon we were surrounded
By a crowd of passers-by.

Education is what remains after one has forgotten

On our school trip to Scarborough
There was really quite a do
When Hazel's hat blew out to sea
And Simon lost a shoe,
And David dropped his flask of soup
Which rolled right off the pier
And landed on the coastguard
Who happened to be near.
Then the coastguard started shouting
When it hit him with a thwack,
And when David said, 'I'm sorry, mate,
Could you pass my thermos back?'

On our school trip to Scarborough
We all ate tons and tons
Of sticky rock and sandwiches
And jellied eels and buns,

And when the coach left Scarborough
Sam was sick on Chris
And Chris was sick on Wayne and Paul
And they were sick on Miss.
Then everyone was shouting
All the children and Miss Phipps
Until Jason asked the driver,
'Can we stop for fish and chips?'

On our school trip to Scarborough
It wasn't that much fun,
Nothing really happened,
And we never saw the sun.
We couldn't do a lot of things
Because of all the rain,
But if I have the chance next year
I'd love to go again!

I was on teaching practice at a primary school in Huddersfield. The head teacher asked me to join him and a party of children for a day trip to the coast. I assumed that the day out would be of an educational nature, that we would be visiting churches together and learning about the geography of the coast. I was soon disabused when the coach pulled into the car park at

what one has learned in school. — Albert Einstein

Bridlington. The head teacher stood at the front of the bus and told the children to explore the town, behave themselves and return to the coach at 3 o'clock. When they were back at school, he told me, they would be asked to write about their experience. I then accompanied him for lunch at a fish and chip café. Just before the designated time we sauntered back to the coach to find all the children lined up and ready for the trip home.

The school where I worked joined up with the neighbouring primary for a residential week in a hotel near the coast. The head teacher of the other school was a bit of a martinet and liked the sound of her own voice. During the week I would get up early and jog along the pebbly beach outside this head teacher's bedroom window. Before breakfast on the second morning she was in an angry mood as she addressed the children.

'Some silly person has been running up and down on the beach outside my window, making a dreadful noise crunching on the pebbles and waking me up. Who is it?'

I raised a hand. 'Sorry,' I said in the voice of a naughty child.

Ben Carter

I took a party of teenagers to Paris over the Easter holidays. We stayed in a small hotel outside the city. The youngsters were warned to behave themselves, the boys not to go into the girls'

A good teacher has been defined as one who makes himself

rooms and vice versa. They were told that lights out was at ten o'clock. At the appointed hour I patrolled the corridors making sure they had obeyed my instruction. In one room I could see the lights shining under the door. I rapped sharply on the wood and shouted.

'I said lights out at ten o'clock! Please do as I say!'

Back came the reply, 'Madam, I shall turn the lights off when I see fit.'

The room was occupied by a guest.

Maggie Talbot

When you were brought up in beautiful countryside you could be excused for sometimes taking it all for granted. But if, like me, you spent your childhood in a mill town in the Heavy Woollen District of the West Riding, you appreciate every minute you can muster in places such as the Yorkshire Dales. Not that I didn't enjoy my early days in Heckmondwike and Batley where typical Yorkshire friendliness, humour and honesty abounds. And, actually, if you could strip away the area's eighteenth- and nineteenth-century industrialisation you'd see many hills and dales as grand and picturesque as many places further north.

Several generations ago my ancestors were farmers on those rugged Pennine hills before they decided, through necessity, to

progressively unnecessary. — Thomas J Carruthers

Teaching consists of equal parts perspiration,

head into the valleys in search of work in the thriving mill towns. Thanks to the foresight of pioneering teachers in the 1960s I was introduced to the great outdoors through the Duke of Edinburgh Awards scheme, which was designed to make ignorant oiks like me from less wealthy areas become better citizens. Dedicated teachers from 'the school on the hill' in Batley, encouraged by the headmaster Mr Locke, gave up their spare time to take groups away to the Hut, at Stainforth Force in Ribblesdale. The Hut was, I later learned, a former cricket pavilion transported from Heckmondwike and placed by permission of the local farmer in the middle of a field near the impressive falls.

In its early days the Hut had no running water, no electricity, some rudimentary bedding and a 'box' outside representing a toilet. The dormitory was at first very basic and we often camped in the field. I distinctly remember those dark nights, hearing the real sounds of nature for the first time. This thirteen-year-old would stick his head out of the tent opening, and stare into the blackness of a Dales night. I'd never known such darkness, growing up on a town centre estate with its yellow street lighting and row upon row of housing. The town hall clock struck every fifteen minutes, drunks stumbled home, the neighbours would argue, and dogs scavenged among the dustbins.

But in the Dales I could hear trees rustling and the Ribble

---

inspiration and resignation. — Susan Ohanian

rushing over the bedrock. In the distance was the rumble of water tumbling over the foss. I listened to an owl for the first time and the occasional bleating of a lamb checking the location of its mum.

During the day we took off on the rope swing and dangled briefly before plunging into the freezing river. We ventured high on to heather-clad hills, breathed clean air and marvelled at the vastness of open countryside and seemingly endless drystone walls. I don't remember feeling any aches or pains as we trudged over bleak fells — okay, I was a tad fitter and several stones lighter then — and took in views over an unfamiliar landscape for us townies.

My parents never had a car so the journey to the Hut was itself an adventure. We travelled the forty-five miles from home on an ancient single-decker bus which rarely went more than 25 mph. It always smelt of cheese and onion crisps. We stopped at the Tomato Dip in Skipton to let the bus have a breather and give the teachers a break from listening to a busful of excited boys.

Those days ignited a passion for the countryside in many of us, and eventually I moved in the opposite direction to my forefathers, heading out of the town and into the countryside for my employment. Without the vision and dedication of those teachers from the 1960s my life could have been so much different.

Paul Jackson

Education is simply the soul of a society as it passes from

SCHOOL TRIP

The great green shiny monster stands still,
Buffed and burnished,
A cold exhibit in a vast museum.
Never again will it rattle down the rails,
Hissing steam, puthering smoke,
Clacking and clattering on the track,
Its whistle shrieking.
There is still the far-off smell of oil and coke,
Slight reminder of when the monster lived and breathed.

'Come along daydreamer,' says my teacher,
'Your worksheet's incomplete.'
And so I count the rivets on the engine
And estimate the length of a carriage.

one generation to another. — G K Chesterton

Chapter Nine

AND THE PRIZE FOR ...

I was presenting the prizes at a girls' high school. The headmistress, a formidable woman, sat next to me on the stage. One student had achieved outstanding results in her A-Levels. When I asked her where she was continuing her studies, she told me at a college in Oxford. I had been at school with one of the lecturers at the college and said I wondered if she had come across him. It turned out he was her tutor. I continued to chat with her about the subject she would be taking.

The headmistress, keen for me to move on, caught my attention, tapped her wristwatch and nodded knowingly to make me shut up. However, I continued to talk to the student, much to the amusement of the audience. At the reception later the chairman of governors, a canon at the cathedral, approached me. 'You know,' he said smiling, 'in the whole history of the school it is the first occasion the speaker has ignored the headmistress on her own stage.'

Some students drink at the fountain of knowledge.

'And the prize for the best attendance this year goes to William Webster.'

(Silence)

'To William Webster.'

(Silence)

'Is William Webster here?'

'No sir, he hasn't turned up!'

Overheard by a parent speaking to her husband at speech day when she saw the headmaster striding on to the stage in his academic gown and mortar board.

'And you say that I wear funny hats.'

'I have to say,' said the chairman of governors to the parents and students at speech day, 'that the headmaster and I were very disappointed by the report of the school inspectors. Indeed when we read the report we were most upset and disappointed by some of the critical comments which we felt were unfounded. Not to put too fine a point on it, we felt we were standing at the edge of a precipice. However, we are moving forward with confidence.'

Others just gargle. — E C McKenzie

The lady mayor, a large woman wearing a rather tight-fitting, pale-blue suit and impressive gold chain, was to present the prizes at the speech day. She was a cheerful, confident and friendly woman who made a point of chatting to the students when they came up on to the stage to receive their awards.

As she bent over a table to pick up a silver cup she broke wind. There is nothing more guaranteed to get young people laughing, and the students broke into peals of laughter much to the embarrassment of the headmaster, whose face took on a vivid shade of red.

Madam mayor handled it superbly and, laughing herself, she walked to the lectern, leaned over and said, 'Hark at me.'

'And now,' said the headmaster at the speech day, 'could we all close our eyes and the chaplain will lead us in a moment of silent prayer.'

At the speech day, the headmaster wore a gown with an ostentatious hood lined in white fur.

'So when were you at the University of Alaska sir?' asked a mischievous sixth former.

test first, the lesson afterward. — Vernon Law

One rather pompous headmaster informed the parents at speech day that he was like the captain of a ship, standing proudly on the bridge, scanning the horizon, heading for the land of opportunity and the harbour of success. 'Sometimes,' he said, 'we are buffeted by the stormy gusts of educational change. Sometimes we are carried off course by the cold currents of government policy. Sometimes we face the hurricanes and gales of school inspection. Sometimes a heavy downpour of yet more documents from the Ministry of Education inundates us. Sometimes we are becalmed by the shortage of the necessary resources. Yet we always keep a steady course, with a firm hand on the tiller, for the land of opportunity and the harbour of success.'

The headmaster paused to sweep his hand before him. 'You know well, students,' he said, 'the name of this, our ship, a name that stands for history, for tradition and for the highest possible standards. What is the name of this, our ship, I ask?'

The headmaster's eyes came to rest on a small boy in the front row who stared up from behind thick-lensed glasses. 'Yes, you, boy,' the headmaster commanded. 'Tell us the name of this ship of ours.'

'Is it the Titanic, sir?' enquired the boy.

The mind is not a vessel to be filled,

Chapter Ten

EENY, MEENY, MINY, MO

CONKERS
Miss Cawthorne says I can't play conkers anymore.
She says it's far too dangerous.
That I could get a bit of conker in my eye
And I'd have to go to hospital
And that I might lose my sight.
'Conkers are banned!' she said.
I told her that I wear glasses,
So there's not much chance
Of getting a bit of conker in my eye.
Miss Cawthorne sent me to the head teacher for being cheeky.

On one school inspection I asked two boys in the playground why they were wearing goggles.

'They're safety glasses,' one boy told me.

---

but a fire to be kindled. — Plutarch

Kids don't remember what you try to teach them.

'Why are you wearing them?' I asked.
'Conkers.'
'Conkers?' I repeated.
'We have to wear these safety glasses if we play conkers,' the boy told me.
''Cos you could get a bit of conker in your eye,' added the other, 'and then the school could get done.'
'No win, no fee,' said his friend, nodding.

Girls spent their playtimes skipping or playing hopscotch, the boys either kicking a football, playing marbles on the bit of grass or had conker contests. One of the tricks in getting a killer conker is to get ones with sharp edges. The big round fat ones are soon destroyed. Then you soak it in vinegar overnight and then bake it in the oven to harden the shell. Seasoned conker winners used a piece of twine and aimed to break the opponent's string.

When his opponent's conker fell on the ground he would stamp on it. Often a fight ensued.

J M Williams

In the playground during the late 1950s and early 1960s we played — or rather, were made to play — a game called British Bulldogs. I think it often constituted the PE lesson of the day, although I doubt it was ever part of any official curriculum.

They remember what you are. — Anon

Perhaps the teachers just believed it helped us let off steam. It certainly wouldn't be allowed under current Health & Safety rules, especially on the steep, hard-surfaced playground of the former Healey Primary School near the Batley-Heckmondwike border in the West Riding of Yorkshire.

I'm sure there are many variations of the game but from what I remember the rules were simple:

One child stands in the middle of the play area.

The rest stand in the top safe area against the wall.

Whoever is 'It' shouts 'Bulldogs!'

The group charge down to the wall at the other end of the playground.

The one who is 'It' tries to touch as many people as possible as they run by.

Those touched have to stay in the middle.

When 'Bulldogs!' is again shouted, the remaining group have to try to make it back to the top wall without being touched.

And so on until only one competitor is left, who then becomes the 'Bulldog' for the next game.

I don't know the tally of sprained wrists, twisted ankles or grazed knees but the game proved to be a good grounding for budding rugby league players if nothing else.

Paul Jackson

Educating the mind without educating

the heart is no education at all. — *Aristotle*

We made our own amusements when we were children. The girls would gather in the playground at the morning break and several long skipping ropes would be produced. I still recall the skipping rhymes:

> *Up the ladder and down the wall,*
> *Penny an hour will serve us all.*
> *You buy butter and I'll buy flour*
> *And we'll have a pudding in half an hour.*
> *With — salt, mustard, vinegar, pepper.*
>
> *Spanish lady turn right round,*
> *Spanish lady touch the ground,*
> *Spanish lady do the high kicks,*
> *Spanish lady do the splits.*
>
> *Black currant, red currant, raspberry tart,*
> *Tell me the name of your sweetheart*
> *A, B, C, D …*

I care not what subject is taught, if only it be taught well. — T H Huxley

We also played hopscotch. There were rhymes for this too.

> *Sister Sarah died in sin,*
> *Dig a hole and put her in.*
> *Dig it deep and dig it narrow*
> *Dig it like an old wheelbarrow.*
> *Set a cup upon a rock,*
> *Put the porridge in the pot.*

Sometimes the boys, bored with playing football or piggyback, would try and stop our games and try and steal our skipping rope or interrupt us when we were playing hopscotch.

Edith Palmer

I remember playing hopscotch as a child. There were lots of rhymes but I only recall the one:

> *Matthew, Mark, Luke and John,*
> *Hold the horse till I leap on;*
> *When I leapt on I could not ride,*
> *I fell off and split my side.*

Jackie Wells

You can never be overdressed or overeducated. — Oscar Wilde

Chapter Eleven

TAKING TO THE STAGE

Young people should have the experience of performing in plays. It is a great disappointment that in some schools drama has been marginalised in the curriculum in favour of more 'useful subjects'. Those of us who have taken part in school plays and directed them know only too well the value of drama when young people can gain in confidence, develop their spoken English and work together. School plays are also great fun.

I remember seeing a brilliant production of *Anne of Green Gables* at a secondary school I was inspecting. The lead part of Anne, played by a plump, red-faced girl with protuberant blue eyes, was undertaken with great enthusiasm and confidence. Dressed in a bright blue and yellow gingham smock, she dominated the stage. After the performance I was taken by the head of the drama department and the play's director to meet members of the cast.

'You were very confident,' I told the girl who had played the lead, 'and did very well to remember all those words. It was a really impressive performance.'

In all the flowers of all the tomorrows are the seeds of today. — Chinese proverb

'I do a lot of drama actually,' she informed me loftily. 'I go to a Saturday stage school and have a main part in *Annie* next week at the local theatre.' She was already well on her way to become a drama queen, I thought.

Then I caught sight of the pale, slight girl who had delivered the opening lines of the play.

'You were excellent,' I told her.

'I only had a few lines,' replied the child, smiling coyly.

'Ah,' I said, 'but you were the first person to speak and it was you who set the scene. We heard every word clearly and if I had an Oscar to award — you know, the prizes that very famous actors sometimes get — well, I would give it to you.'

'That was kind of you, Mr Phinn,' said the head of the drama department later, 'and if you only knew what that will do for that young lady's confidence. She is such a shy little thing and it took some persuading to get her to take part.'

'She deserved an Oscar,' I said. 'Anyone who could go on to the stage, before all the other actors, beneath all the bright lights, in front of a hundred people and deliver such lines without making one mistake, deserves an Oscar.'

The teacher looked at me quizzically. 'In what way?' she asked.

I consulted my programme. 'I wrote down the words she had to say,' I said, 'and I guess many of us would have had some difficulty declaiming them with such clarity.' I read the lines: "Is Farmer Hart's farm far from here?"

I am not a teacher, but an awakener. — Robert Frost

The task of the modern educator is not to cut

I was told some years ago by Graham Allen, the distinguished former drama adviser for Wakefield, about a school production of *Macbeth*. The sixth former playing the lead was another massively confident and rather self-satisfied young actor. Seyton, an officer attending on Macbeth, was played by a small eleven-year-old who only had a very few lines to deliver. In Act V he comes on stage to inform Macbeth, 'The queen, my lord, is dead,' whereupon the devastated king declaims his famous monologue. On the Thursday night the little boy's relations took up the entire front row and when he made his appearance there was an audible noise from his fans. 'Look, it's our Darren,' came a voice from the audience. Seyton, aware that his family was there, developed his part somewhat and began rubbing his eyes, wailing piteously and beating his breast. 'The queen, my lord, oh, oh, the poor queen is dead. She's dead! Dead! Dead!' Then to applause he exited stage right.

Macbeth was far from happy after the performance. 'Say your line and get off,' he shouted at the boy, 'and cut out all that other stuff because if you start that tomorrow night I'll kick you off the stage!'

It was the last night. Macbeth, alone on the battlements, sees his world crumbling about him.

'Wherefore was that cry?' he asks plaintively.

Enter Seyton.

'The queen, my lord,' he announces, 'is making a remarkable recovery.' (I guess it is not true but it makes a wonderful story.)

---

down jungles, but to irrigate deserts. — C S Lewis

Worried about the use of the word 'bloody' in the school production of *Macbeth* the head teacher suggested to the young actor playing the part of King Duncan that he should substitute something for the offending word in the line: 'What bloody man is that?

The boy duly obliged and on the night asked: 'Who's that daft bugger then?'

I witnessed a wonderful Yorkshire version of *Hamlet* performed in a school in Sheffield by the senior students. As an introduction to the play the teacher had transposed the original into Yorkshire dialect.

Two boys ambled towards each other at the front of the room, hands thrust deep in their pockets.

'Hey up, 'Amlet.'

'Hey up, 'Oratio, what's tha doin' 'ere?'

'Nowt much. 'Ow abaat thee then, 'Amlet? I ant seen thee for a bit.'

'Nay, I'm not that champion, 'Oratio, if t' truth be towld.'

'Whay, 'Amlet, what's oop?'

'Mi dad's deead, mi mam's married mi uncle and mi girlfriend does nowt but nag, nag, nag. I tell thee, 'Oratio, I'm weary wi' it.'

'Aye, tha's not far wrong theer, 'Amlet, She's gorra reight gob on 'er, that Hophelia. Teks after 'er owld man.'

The highlight of the performance was following the most famous of

Shakespeare's soliloquies:
   'To be or not to be, that's t' question.
   Whether 'tis nobbler in t' mind
   To suffer t' slings and 'arras of outrageeous fowtune
   Or to tek harms agin a sea of troubles.
   And by opposin', end 'em.'
   Ophelia enters.
   'Hey up, our 'Amlet, talkin' to theesen ageean, People'll think tha'r tapped in t' head.'
   'Shut thee clack, thee.'
   'That's no way to talk to yer girlfriend, 'Amlet. We're supposed to be coourtin'.'
   'Not any more we're not.'
   'Tha knaas what, 'Amlet, tha's a reight mardybum these days. What's up wi' thee?'
   'Nowt's up wi' me. Gerron ooam an' stop thee mitherin'.'
   'Ooooh, 'Amlet.'
   'I've done wi' wimmin. Tha's all t' same. Me mam's a tart and I've doubts about thee an all.'
   'Ooooh, 'Amlet.'
   'And geeore rooarin'.'

to miserable uncertainty. — Mark Twain

The part of Fagin in the school production of the musical *Oliver!* was taken by the deputy head teacher, a talented actor and someone with a great sense of humour. The problem for the producer was that he would not learn his lines and frequently went off script adding asides and making comments. This threw some of the other actors who waited nervously for their cues.

On the last night, Fagin was encouraged to ad-lib by a large woman on the front row with a loud and infectious laugh. She too was wont to add to the drama. After young Oliver sang the heartfelt 'Where is Love?' she said rather volubly, 'Aaaah bless him.' When Bill Sikes hits Nancy she could be heard saying 'My goodness. The brute!' The deputy head (aka Fagin) sang the final number 'I'm Reviewing the Situation'. He then looked at the woman on the front row. 'Could you take on a dirty old man?' he asked.

'I've got one love. He's sitting next to me.'

I directed the comic opera *The Pirates of Penzance* in an inner city, multi-racial school. In one of the scenes the major general enters the stage surrounded by his many daughters. The girls playing the parts of the daughters were from many different cultures and backgrounds — Indian, Pakistani, Chinese, Polish and Nepalese. One parent, sitting on the front row and observing the great variety of ethnicities, remarked rather audibly, 'He's been putting it about a bit.'

Education is the ability to listen to almost anything without

I observed the rehearsal for the school play in a Roman Catholic primary school. The play told the story of St John the Baptist. The teacher producing the drama was in full flow when I entered the hall. On stage a large, shaven-headed boy holding a paper crown and a large plastic sword was staring impassively at the teacher.

'Now, Herod,' said the teacher, 'when Salome brings on John the Baptist's head, you look very sad. You really didn't want to have him killed but had to keep your promise to Salome that she could have anything she wanted.' The teacher caught sight of a small boy at the side of the hall, holding a large papier-mâché plate. 'John,' she said irritably, 'where is the head?'

'Pardon, Miss?' asked the child.

'Where is John the Baptist's head? It should be on the platter.'

'I haven't got it, Miss,' replied the child. 'No one has given it to me.'

'Peter,' the teacher instructed another child, 'go to the staff room and fetch the bleeding head.'

The boy returned moments later with the head teacher.

In one school production of *A Midsummer Night's Dream* the boy playing the part of Bottom displayed remarkable aplomb when the stage set collapsed behind him. As the other young actors froze and the audience laughed, he took centre stage and announced: 'Prithee, look you at that forsooth. Yon wall has collapseth.' Then as an aside he added, 'Zoounds, that's the trouble when thou employeth cowboy builders.'

---

losing your temper or your self-confidence. — Robert Frost

As a schoolboy I was given the part of Oberon in *A Midsummer Night's Dream*. I cannot say I was all that keen when I was cast as the King of the Fairies but there was one real benefit. I got to kiss Titania, the Queen of the Fairies, who was played by the delectable Shirley Ramsey. Shirley was a most attractive girl — shapely and elegant — and I was very much looking forward to the scene when she lay prone on her bed of flowers and I would awaken her from her dream with a kiss.

The play was well-received and with each performance my amorous scene with Shirley became more adventurous and exploratory. On the first night it was a peck on the cheek but by the time of the final performance, I really got into my stride and gave her a great smacker full on the lips. Her eyes shot open. 'Knock that off!' she hissed. 'You're a sex maniac!'

THE REHEARSAL
This morning, children, we have a special visitor in school.
He's sitting at the back of the hall.
His name is Mr Leatherboy and he's a school inspector
Come to watch the rehearsal for our Nativity Play.
I am sure he will leave us very much impressed.
I don't think he will be very much impressed
By what you are doing, Malcolm Biggerdyke.
Donkeys don't roll about on the floor making silly noises,
Now do they? They stand up straight and pay attention.

Education is the most powerful weapon which you

Justine, don't do that with Baby Jesus, dear,
And Philip, please stop fiddling with the frankincense.
How do you mean you've got your finger stuck in the hole in the lid?
Well how did you manage to do that?
My goodness, that was a silly thing to do, wasn't it?
Well, if it went in it must come out, wiggle it about a bit.
No, I don't mean your bottom, wiggle your finger about.
He doesn't need your help thank you very much, Harry.
Yes, I know you are only trying to be helpful.
Just leave the lid alone and put your crown on straight.
Justine, I have asked you not to do that with Baby Jesus,
And Gavin, will you stop that immediately.
Crooks are for holding sensibly and not for swinging about.
You will have someone's eye out.
Angela dear, I really don't think the Angel of the Lord
Would wipe her nose on her sleeve, now would she?
Use a tissue. Well go and get one from Mrs Tricklebank.
Tyrone, palm trees stand still, they do not wander about the stage.
Go back and stand on your spot and don't wave your fronds about.
Justine, I shall not tell you again not to do that with Baby Jesus.
Jonathan Jones, why are you pulling that silly face?
One day the wind will change and it will stay like that.
Yes, I know you didn't want to be Joseph,

can use to change the world. — Nelson Mandela

Yes, I know you wanted to be the grumpy innkeeper,
But there are some things in life many of us don't want to do
And we just have to grin and bear it and not pull silly faces.
Duane, I did ask you not to wear those red trainers.
Herod wouldn't be wearing shoes which light up and flash
Now would he? No, you can't wear your wellingtons.
What is it Justine? Well, I did tell you not to do that with Baby Jesus.
Put him back in the crib and leave him alone.
I am sure we will fix his head back on before the performance.
Well, I think we are about ready to start, Mr Leatherboy.
Oh dear, he appears to have gone.

Children must be taught how to think, not what to think. — Margaret Mead

ACKNOWLEDGEMENTS

I am immensely grateful to all those people who have generously shared with me their memories of school; and to Mark Whitley and Robert Flanagan of Country Publications for allowing me to write about my very favourite subject: education.

G P

Contributors — p21: John Bassett; p 22: Elizabeth Mary Atkinson; p24: Bernice Ashton; p24, p48, p131, p143: Paul Jackson; p26: Linda Wilson; p27: Arnold Greenwood; p30: Bernard Jenkins; p40: Philip Graves; p40: Michael Pratt; p41: Debbie Saunders; p43: Gerard Smith; p43: Thomas White; p44: Barry McCann; p44: Gerard Basset; p44: Gary Wilson; p45: George Hutchinson; p48: Ernest Thompson; p55: Malcolm Wright; p55: Geraldine O'Connor; p55: Auberon Waugh; p56: Frances Davies; p56: Norman Ford; p58: Leonard Morris; p58: Martin Bowler; p59: Marlene Johnson; p59: Annette Jones; p60: Marton Barber; p60: Norman Foster; p60: Alison Riley; p62: Andrew Thompson; p63: T J Murphy; p63: FD; p63: Simon Brown; p65: CJ; p65: Janice Walker; p65, p90, p93: Diane French; p67: Jack Drake; p67: C J Black; p72: Angela Stringer; p77: Eleanor Radcliffe; p81: F Norman; p91: Daniel McNeil; p91: Christine Mason; p91: CP; p93: John Metcalfe; p107: Michael Brown; p126: Janice Moore; p130: Ben Carter; p131: Maggie Talbot; p143: J M Williams; p146: Edith Palmer; p146: Jackie Wells.*

Photography — Cover: Two youngsters sharing books at a school on the Hebridean Islands. (Photo Thurston Hopkins/Getty Images); p10: Primary Class. (Photo Bert Hardy/Getty Images); p16: 15th October 1955: Two young children starting the new term at French-speaking day school, Le Lycee Francais in Kensington; London. Original Publication: Picture Post 8051: A French School In London: pub. 1955 (Photo by John Chillingworth/Picture Post/Getty Images); p28: 1950 Nursery school children playing in a sand pit. (Photo by William Vanderson/Fox Photos/Getty Images); p61: Class Work. (Photo Bert Hardy/Getty Images); p68: Naughty Schoolboy. (Photo Hans Bethlem/Getty Images); p80: Copycat. (Photo Haywood Magee/Getty Images); p86: Father looking at his son's report card. (Photo SuperStock;

Inc.); p109: 14th March 1953. A teacher taking a class at Belmont Secondary Boys' School, Harrow Weald. Original Publication: Picture Post 6442: 3,000,000 Illiterates: Why?: pub. 1953. (Photo by George Douglas/Picture Post/Getty Images); p115: Maths Test. Photo Vagn Hansen/Getty Images); p132: 18th June 1949: Students of the Aberdovey Outward Bound School study maps on a walk on Cader Idris. Original Publication: Picture Post 4815: A Sea School's Hike: pub. 1949 (Photo by Haywood Magee/Picture Post/Getty Images); p139: February 1962: Headmaster Sydney Baxter addresses pupils at the William Ellis School in Highgate, London. (Photo by Chris Ware/Keystone Features/Getty Images); p142: 1st January 1944: A group of girls skipping in the playground of Llansamlet School in Wales. Original Publication: Picture Post 1448: Education In The Valley,pub. 1944 (Photo by Leonard McCombe/Picture Post/Getty Images); p145: Play time at St Mary's school in Boston, Lincolnshire, with a teacher watching the children playing games during a break, circa 1953. (Photo by Popperfoto/Getty Images); p150: Nativity Play. (Photo Raymond Kleboe/Getty Images).

Publication acknowledgements — p8: Report on the school attached to Bar Chapel, Cowling, from Cowling a Moorland Parish *by Cowling Local History Society, 1980.*

Every effort has been made to track down copyright holders. The publishers would be pleased to receive details of any errors and ommissions, to be corrected in subsequent editions.